Theories, Models and Concepts in Ancient History

The place of 'theory' in the study of the past is controversial. Some historians believe that the use of ideas and concepts from disciplines like economics and sociology produces anachronistic and distorted accounts. Others argue that all historians use generalisations about human nature and the workings of society – in other words, some sort of 'theory' – but that most are unconscious of the assumptions on which their accounts of the past depend, a position with its own set of problems.

Neville Morley's book offers the first accessible guide for students to how theories, models and concepts have been applied to ancient history. It shows readers how they can use theory to interpret historical evidence for themselves, as well as to evaluate the work of others.

The book concludes with a survey of key ideas and theories on a wide range of ancient historical topics, including society and economy, the environment, gender and sexuality, and myth and rationality. A helpful annotated guide to further reading on all the topics covered is also provided.

Neville Morley is Senior Lecturer in Ancient History at the University of Bristol. His previous books include *Writing Ancient History* (1999) and, as editor, *Ancient History: Key Themes and Approaches* (Routledge, 2000).

Approaching the Ancient World

Theories, Models and Concepts in Ancient History

Neville Morley

Routledge
Taylor & Francis Group

LONDON AND NEW YORK

First published 2004
by Routledge
2 Park Square, Milton Park, Abingdon, Oxon, OX14 4RN

Simultaneously published in the USA and Canada
by Routledge
270 Madison Ave, New York NY 10016

Routledge is an imprint of the Taylor & Francis Group

Transferred to Digital Printing 2007

© 2004 Neville Morley

Typeset in Baskerville by Prepress Projects Ltd, Perth, Scotland

British Library Cataloguing in Publication Data
A catalogue record for this book is available from the British Library

Library of Congress Cataloging in Publication Data
Morley, Neville.
Theories, models, and concepts in ancient history / Neville Morley.
    p. cm. -- (Approaching the ancient world)
Includes bibliographical references and index.
1. History, Ancient–Historiography. 2. History, Ancient–Philosophy.
3. Historiography. I. Title. II. Series.
D56.M6598 2004
930'.0–dc22
2003023939

ISBN   0–415–24876–0 (hbk)
           0–415–24877–9 (pbk)

Publisher's Note
The publisher has gone to great lengths to ensure the quality of this
reprint but points out that some imperfections in the original
may be apparent

Contents

Acknowledgements

My first encounters with Fernand Braudel, Clifford Geertz and the like, as part of a compulsory 'General Historical Problems' paper at university, were marked by incomprehension, boredom and a moderately catastrophic performance in the exam. This experience has since provided me with an invaluable psychological defence mechanism when my students have produced similar reactions to 'theory': the value of such encounters is, more often than not, recognised only in retrospect, and I can now see how much I owe to Peter Burke and Gwyn Prins for starting me on this particular path of development as a historian. Since then I have been pulled, goaded, cajoled and generally helped on my way by innumerable people, of whom I can list only a few whose names spring immediately to mind: teachers (Paul Cartledge, Peter Garnsey, Keith Hopkins, Jonathan Walters), fellow students (Jonathan Hall, Vedia Izzet, Andrew Kreider, Jeremy Tanner), past and present colleagues at Bristol (Catharine Edwards, Sitta von Reden, Vanda Zajko) and my own students (Daniella Bowker, Amelia Fishburn, Alex Hobbs, Geraint Osborn, Alan Smith and Jack Talbot, among many). This book, like its predecessor *Writing Ancient History*, is intended to repay a little of my intellectual debt by providing future generations of ancient history students with a sort of guidebook to the world of 'theory'; in part to stop them feeling too lost, and in part to encourage them to visit it in the first place by introducing its noted monuments and other attractions.

On the personal side, I have received great support and encouragement during some difficult times from Richard Buxton, Gillian Clark and Bob Fowler. I owe my health and happiness above all to Anne, to Angharad, to Jill Glover, without whose help I might not have written another book, and to Basil, who did his level best to sabotage the writing of this one.

Chapter 1

Approaches

The problem of theory

> Within the discipline of ancient history, grown to a stunted maturity under the paternalistic aegis of classical philology, approaches to history that stress the techniques and methodologies of the social sciences (e.g., primacy of theory, model building, conceptual sophistication, quantification) rather than those of the mainstream tradition (e.g., linguistic categorization, literary source criticism, citation of authority) must expect to meet with more than a slight suspicion of illegitimacy.[1]

The place of 'theory' in ancient history remains controversial. Its advocates (normally advocates of one particular theoretical approach rather than of theory in general) insist that un- or undertheorised historical accounts are inadequate, because they depend on a set of implicit and problematic assumptions masquerading as 'common sense'. Its opponents maintain that any account of antiquity using modern concepts and theories is illegitimate and misleading, as the evidence has been corrupted and distorted with anachronism (and, more often than not, a political agenda). Most present-day historians find themselves somewhere in the middle, at risk of attack from both sides: recognising that they should include at least some discussion of the key terms and ideas used in their work, and often making use of material from outside ancient history to illuminate their studies, but regarding 'theory' as something ancillary to the real business of ancient history, something alien and even threatening.

The emotions that this debate continues to arouse – anger and anxiety on one side, fervent enthusiasm on the other – make it clear that this is not a purely technical, methodological issue. The question of whether and how ancient historians should make use of modern theories and concepts in interpreting ancient material in fact raises fundamental questions about ancient history as a discipline and about the status and authority of its accounts of the past. 'Theory' – economics, for example, or Marxism – seems to promise a great deal, claiming to provide a true understanding of how the world *really* works and to reveal the underlying logic and pattern behind the apparent chaos of past and present events. It seems to offer, in some cases, the possibility that history might aspire to the status of a kind of science, the most prestigious and authoritative form of knowledge in the modern West. However, the promise is also a threat: history is to acquire this new status and authority by effectively ceasing to be itself and becoming a branch of some other discipline, whether economics, sociology, anthropology or literary theory. Traditional practices are to be abandoned as inadequate; existing accounts of the past must be repudiated as at best lacking in intellectual rigour and explanatory power and at worst compromised and tainted by dubious philosophical, political and ethical assumptions. For the professional ancient historian with a certain amount invested in existing disciplinary structures and traditions, or for the student who is investing time, effort and money in acquiring the historian's traditional knowledge and skills, some anxiety in the face of such claims and assertions seems quite understandable.

For polemical purposes, one might contrast 'theory' both with 'practice' and with 'reality'. Historians, it may be argued, learn their craft through practice and imitation, through the study of how other historians work and through developing historical arguments and interpretations of their own, not through studying abstract philosophical ideas about the construction of historical knowledge. Their knowledge of the past is based on direct contact with the actual evidence in all its variety, rather than on trying to force a past reality to conform to abstract models and questionable prior assumptions. Theory, on this reading, is too simplistic and abstract, since it attempts to reduce the complexity of the real world, of human motivation and of history itself, to a single principle or a few alleged laws. Indeed, traditional historical accounts might claim to be *more* scientific than theoretical ones, because they are firmly grounded in the evidence. At the same time, theory appears unnecessarily complicated, as it demands that historians should adopt a highly specialised technical vocabulary in place of plain English and should learn a whole new subject on top of – or, worse, instead of – basic historical skills and knowledge of the evidence. For most historians, scepticism about theory's claims – surely reality is always more complicated? – leaves them with little motivation to acquire more than a superficial familiarity with some key terms and ideas. It is left to just a few individuals of questionable intellectual tendencies to undergo an almost religious conversion to the cult of theory, abandoning the complexities of real life in favour of belief in a single Truth that purports to explain everything.

I suspect that this account will ring true with a significant number of practising historians and students. It is not, however, the only way of defining 'theory' and characterising its relation to history. Rather than being placed in opposition to historical practice and past reality, theory can be seen as intrinsically bound up with both of them: as the set of ideas and assumptions that inform and govern historians' practices and with and through which we interpret the world. Under this definition, not only do all historians possess some sort of 'theory', but historical knowledge would be impossible without it: 'theory' is what enables us to make sense of evidence and use it to create an account of the past. Historical sources do not 'speak' or present us with their intrinsic meaning and significance; rather, we give them meaning and significance by interpreting them, considering them in the context of existing knowledge and understanding, making connections with other pieces of evidence, using them to build up and then modify a wider picture of the past.[2] In this process of interpretation, our choices and judgements – What is the appropriate context for this piece of evidence? Is this a plausible connection? Is this a valid interpretation? – are influenced by a wide variety of ideas and assumptions: philosophical premises and methodological rules of thumb, the conventions of the discipline and personal intuition, elaborate theoretical concepts and the set of cultural assumptions about human nature and the like that we have learnt to regard as 'common sense', things apparently so obviously true that they are scarcely worth discussing. That is to say, our interpretations are based on – and, essentially, made possible by – some sort of 'theory', however vague and eclectic. The fact that the ideas governing historians' practices and interpretations are frequently unsystematic, largely implicit and often quite unconscious and unquestioned does not lessen their importance. The advocates of 'theory' are not seeking to replace 'non-theoretical' accounts of the past with 'theoretical' ones but to favour histories in which the theoretical assumptions are explicit and coherent over those in which historians are largely oblivious to the ideas that are influencing their interpretations.

In a way, therefore, it all depends on what one means by 'theory'. The debate about theory in ancient history has been complicated by the fact that different participants have had different conceptions of what it was they were discussing. It is the nature of such controversial 'keywords' that they have a wide range of reference, are heavily laden with ideas and values – and are frequently bound up with the problems that they are being used to discuss.[3] That is to say, definitions are rarely, if ever, neutral. Defining 'theory' as something opposed to both practice and reality, something external to history, and restricting the term to such elaborate, self-contained systems of thought as Marxism or economics, can be seen as a strategy that defends traditional historical practices against the claims and criticisms of other approaches. Conversely, characterising *any* set of ideas that influence historical interpretation, however incoherent or inconsistent, as 'theory' carries (and is intended to carry) entirely different implications. By erasing most of the differences between, say, Marxism and conventional historiography, it implies that both approaches embody the sorts of philosophical, political and metaphysical assumptions that are explicit and thus easily criticised in Marxism. That being so, much of the criticism of traditional history from a theoretical point of view is seen to be merited, and it becomes clear that historians do indeed need to review both their practices and their existing accounts of the past. More positively, such a definition suggests that, as 'theory' is not in fact so alien to history, it would not after all be so difficult for ancient historians to reap the benefits of adopting more theoretically informed approaches to their subject.

From this perspective, the subject of 'theory in ancient history' is more than the study of some outré concepts and systems of thought that have been applied to antiquity by one or two eccentrics. The danger of a book such as this, or of a stand-alone unit on 'Approaches to Ancient History', is that it reinforces the idea that 'theory' is something separate from, additional to and even alien to the normal practices of ancient history. On the contrary, the study of 'theory' is the study of historical interpretation in general, the different ways in which historians produce accounts of the past on the basis of the surviving evidence. Complex theoretical systems such as Marxism serve as useful examples for such a study because they highlight the sorts of issues and problems that are common to all historical interpretations but are left implicit, even concealed, in more conventional approaches to ancient history. The 'problem' of theory is not that it is some alien force trying to take over history, but rather that, by convincing themselves that it is and that they are under attack, historians have blinded themselves to the theories that inform their own practices and interpretations. They have also chosen to shut themselves off to ideas and methods that might help to illuminate ancient evidence and produce more interesting and sophisticated – and no less 'real' – interpretations of the past.

Approaches to ancient history

The aims of this book are threefold. First, I want to introduce some of the key concepts, arguments and assumptions of a range of theories that have informed and influenced different accounts of ancient history. Whether or not a student makes use of 'theory' in his or her own work, the fact that some other historians do make use of it means that a certain amount of knowledge of different theories, of how they are used, how they can be recognised and how they might be evaluated, is a vital part of the historian's basic 'toolbox' of skills. I have chosen to arrange the book around different aspects of ancient history (economy, society, culture, mentality) rather than devoting separate chapters to different theories. This does mean that my discussions of such complex theoretical traditions as sociology and structuralism are decidedly limited and superficial, focusing on one or two key ideas rather than attempting to give a complete account of each system of thought. On the other hand, students are most likely to encounter 'theory' in the context of particular debates in ancient history rather than on its own, and it is easier to compare and contrast different theories and to evaluate their strengths and weaknesses by looking at how they have been applied to historical problems rather than by considering them purely in the abstract. The guide to further reading is intended to point students in the direction both of more detailed introductions to different theories and of further examples of their application to ancient history. The choice of topics does show a certain bias towards social and economic history: partly because this is my main area of interest and expertise, but above all because it is in these areas, which the 'social sciences' claim as their domain, that traditional historiography faces the greatest challenges to the validity and authority of its approach to the past and, more positively, that theoretical approaches seem to have the most to offer to ancient historians.

Second, I want to offer this material as the basis for a more general discussion of how historians develop interpretations and construct arguments, and how those interpretations and arguments should be evaluated. As I suggested above, explicitly theoretical approaches to ancient history make good examples for the study of historical interpretation because their assumptions and interpretative strategies are normally quite overt; having studied such approaches, the same techniques and criteria of evaluation can be applied to works the guiding assumptions of which are less obvious (in some cases, even the historian may not be wholly aware of them). Both these aims relate to the skill of critical reading, something that needs to be applied to secondary sources as much as to ancient evidence. As with the interpretation of ancient evidence, this involves more than just having a critical attitude, not accepting what the sources say at face value (though that is clearly important): we need to have a sense of what to look for, of the right questions to ask, of the possible contexts within which the work can be interpreted. Just as we look at Livy in the context of the development of Roman historiography and the establishment of the Principate, and consider his work in relation to other contemporary literature which reinterprets Roman myths and traditions, so we need, for example, to consider the work of M.I. Finley in the context of a debate about the nature of the ancient economy that has been running since the late eighteenth century and to think about its relation to parallel debates in economic theory and anthropology. Few historians are *not* influenced by contemporary ideas and discussions, even if they do not draw on them explicitly; we need to know enough about the wider intellectual context of their work to be able to recognise such influences and evaluate the results.

My third aim is slightly more polemical: to demonstrate the possibilities of a 'theoretical' approach to ancient history as a source of new ideas and new ways of reading the ancient evidence and, thus, as a means of developing a richer understanding of the past. As is doubtless obvious from the fact that I have chosen to write such a book in the first place, my own approach to ancient history is heavily influenced by 'theory'. I begin from the basic assumption that the historian's task is to explain past events, rather than simply to record them, and to understand past society in terms of the underlying structures that shaped people's lives rather than simply describing the diversity of their experiences. We cannot, I believe, avoid interpreting the past in terms of present concepts and concerns; it is surely better to do this consciously and explicitly, aware of the possi-

derived, etic perspective

bility of anachronism and distortion, than to convince ourselves that we can gain direct access to the *real* past, untainted and unmediated by any modern influences. If we accept what one might term the inevitability of anachronism, we can feel free to draw upon all the ideas and concepts that the modern world, with greater resources and above all much greater volumes of evidence, has developed to understand society and the world at large. I am not aiming to promote a particular theory – though I have my preferred approaches, as will probably become evident in the course of this book, however scrupulously I try to be fair in presentation and evaluation – but the advantages of a theoretical approach.

Of course, theoretical ideas and concepts need to be evaluated critically and applied sensitively and with regard to historical context – or at least that is one of my basic theoretical assumptions. For the rest of this chapter, I want to discuss a number of general points relating to the use of such theories, highlighting some of the underlying issues that will recur regularly through the rest of the book. I have taken as a focus for this discussion M.I. Finley's characterisation of the ancient city as a 'consumer city', an idea discussed in a number of his books and in particular in an article of 1977.[4] This is a classic example of an explicitly 'theoretical' approach to a topic in ancient history – 'classic' both in its methodology and in its influence over subsequent studies of ancient urbanism. It is clear evidence of the power of this concept that even twenty-five years later historians find it difficult to study Greek or Roman cities without engaging, however briefly, with Finley's ideas. Indeed, entire academic conferences have been organised with the express aim of getting 'beyond the consumer city' – which suggests that Finley's argument may serve as an example also of some of the potential problems and drawbacks of a theoretically informed approach to ancient history.[5]

Generalisations and comparisons

The outstanding characteristic of 'theoretical' as opposed to 'traditional' approaches to ancient history is their emphasis on the general rather than the particular. Of course, this is a matter of degree and emphasis rather than an absolute distinction: *all* historians aim to draw together individual pieces of evidence to produce a more general account and interpret the evidence on the basis of wider assumptions ('generalisations') about the ancient world and the world in general.[6] However, any historical account can be located on a spectrum between those that focus primarily on the individual event or institution and those that examine events or institutions primarily with the aim of drawing more general conclusions that might be applied to other examples, even to other historical periods. For example, one might study the reign of a particular Roman emperor as something that is interesting in itself, or as a way of understanding the nature of the Principate and the role of emperors, or even in search of transhistorical ideas about leadership and power.[7] In the last accounts, the particular case is interpreted explicitly in terms of a more general theory or concept ('the Principate', 'power') and is of interest primarily in so far as it serves either as evidence to confirm the validity of the general principle or as grounds for modifying and refining it. From this perspective, simply collecting information about a particular case, without any reference to a wider research agenda, does little to advance our understanding of the past.

> In the end, I believe that the history of *individual* ancient towns is a cul-de-sac, given the limits of the available (and potential) documentation, the unalterable condition of the study of ancient history. It is not wholly perverse to see an advantage in the weakness. There is mounting criticism of contemporary urban history for allowing the deluge of data to obscure the questions being asked and their purpose, a danger that the ancient urban historian is happily safe from. But what questions do we wish to ask about the ancient city, whether they can be answered satisfactorily or not? That is the first thing to be clear about, before the evidence is collected, let alone interrogated. If my evaluation of the current situation is a bleak one, that is not because I dislike the questions that are being asked but because I usually fail to discover any questions at all, other than antiquarian ones – how big? how many? what monuments? how much trade? which products?[8]

We have insufficient evidence, according to Finley, to write a proper history of any individual ancient city, even Rome or Pompeii – but in any case that should not be the aim of our studies. Instead, we should be seeking 'to *understand* the place of the town as a pivotal institution in the Graeco-Roman world and its development'.[9] Individual cities are of interest not in themselves but in so far as they tell us something about ancient cities in general, helping us to develop an idea of the place of 'the city' in Greek and Roman society.

Finley's aim is to identify attributes that are common to all, or at least most, ancient cities, and to develop ideas and concepts that can then be applied to any (or at least any 'average' or 'typical') Greek or Roman city. Only if we study individual ancient cities as part of a wider research project like this will we be able to ask the right sorts of questions of the evidence, to yield the right sorts of knowledge and understanding of the past. The failure, in Finley's eyes, of most accounts of ancient cities is that they do not even try to generalise, but simply accrue information related to their subject: this is 'latter-day antiquarianism', in contrast to a properly analytical history.[10]

> There are, to be sure, a growing number of 'histories' of individual towns, Greek and Roman, from the archaic age to the end of antiquity. With scarcely an exception, however, they lack a conceptual focus or scheme.[11]

> Instead of efforts to establish clear patterns of city behaviour through the employment of simplifying assumptions, there has emerged in recent decades a spate of pseudo-histories of ancient cities and regions in which every statement or calculation to be found in an ancient text, every artefact finds a place, creating a morass of unintelligible, meaningless, unrelated 'facts'.[12]

In a 'theoretical' history, the historian's main aim is to identify patterns, trends, rules and laws, underlying structures, overall frameworks and essential features. Such accounts offer a particular sort of knowledge about the past – a way of thinking about it and imagining it, rather than simply information about it. Having dismissed other approaches, Finley does not then attempt to offer a complete account of all aspects of the ancient city but focuses on what he regards as its defining feature, the relationship between the city and its territory. In contrast to the medieval city, the city of producers, that paid for its food supply with goods and services, the ancient city was supported by taxes and rents collected from the producers in the countryside. Moreover, whereas the medieval city was politically as well as economically independent, and hence became a privileged space in which new ideas developed and a new class rose to power, in antiquity town and country were politically united, dominated by the same landowning elite and its values. Hence, it is argued, ancient and medieval cities played very different roles in the economic histories of their times – the one a locus, even a catalyst, for development and growth, the other at best neutral and perhaps even an impediment to change. Of course, the ancient world contained an enormous variety of cities, including some in which trade and manufacture played a more prominent role, but underlying even the thriving business activities and wealth of a place such as Pompeii is its dependence on the produce of its immediate hinterland, gathered in by the elite as taxes and rents: the exploitative relationship that characterises and defines the 'consumer city'.[13]

Whether this sort of approach to history is appealing and stimulating may in the end be a matter of personal preference and temperament: is this the sort of knowledge about the past that we desire? Crudely, do we focus on the innumerable representations of penises at Pompeii because they are exotic and interesting in themselves or because they can tell us something about the economics of Roman prostitution?[14] Do we study Pompeii in and for itself or simply as an example of 'ancient urbanism'? Ian Morris has characterised the crucial difference between the approaches of 'the humanities' and 'the social sciences' as lying in their different aims of 'understanding' and 'explanation': the one emphasises the complexity, detail, richness and variety of human behaviour, the other seeks to identify underlying general principles behind what appears to be undifferentiated randomness.[15] As a result of both inclination and training, many historians tend to follow the path of the humanities, favouring the striking detail and the revealing anecdote; they are suspicious of grand theory precisely because it devalues such details and obscures the differences between individual cases and even between historical periods. For those inclined to theoretical approaches, of course, this is precisely why they should be preferred.

> At the risk of caricaturing complex issues, we might say that in the humanist's eyes, reducing the world to a handful of principles tells us little, because it ignores precisely those things that we most need to understand. In the social scientists' eyes, humanists systematically select on dependent variables, superficially wallowing in particulars rather than seeking explanation.[16]

No historian rejects generalisation altogether, however much he or she focuses on the particular; history – indeed, life in general – would be impossible if we believed that there was never any connection between events or that distinct but similar objects could never be compared. Rather, historians have an individual sense of what sorts of generalisations they are willing to accept and employ and what sort of knowledge of the past they are attempting to produce. When reading a historical work, we need to pay attention to the generalisations that underlie the historian's interpretations – not all of which may be explicit, or even conscious – to evaluate them and to assess their significance. This may provide grounds for rejecting the book's conclusions altogether, if we decide that its assumptions are excessively dubious, or we may modify them in line with our own perspective. For example, Finley's idea of the 'consumer city' is closely bound up with his overall view of the ancient economy as essentially undeveloped (a theory discussed in the next chapter); but it is quite possible to accept that his model does apply to ancient cities while rejecting, or at least qualifying, his pessimistic view of the development of antiquity.[17]

When evaluating general theories and concepts, we can, for the sake of argument, distinguish between two key aspects. The first may be termed the 'breadth' of the generalisation: how large a geographical region, how great an extent of time, how many different facets of human activity does it claim to encompass? Put another way, how vulnerable is any given generalisation to being dismissed as 'sweeping'? The main aim of theory is to show that apparently different situations and societies are in fact comparable. Commonly, this involves metaphors of depth and surface, or foundation and superstructure: the obvious differences between societies are assumed to obscure their underlying similarity. A key point in any such argument is therefore the basis on which this continuity is established. This may be relatively easy in the case of theories that cover a limited aspect of life in a single society; it is more problematic if we wish to extend a theory developed through study of the modern world to other, pre-modern societies. For example, a common criticism of attempts to apply modern economic theory to the ancient world is that they simply assume that a form of behaviour associated with the modern West (namely, a propensity to maximise utility) is actually a universal trait of 'human nature'. It is possible to make a case to justify this assumption and hence to justify the use of the theory, but it cannot be taken for granted that our own beliefs, customs and ideas are universally valid rather than historically and culturally specific. An obvious focus for the evaluation of any given theory is therefore to consider what assumptions of historical continuity are being made in order for it to be used, especially when it is being deployed outside its original context.

Some theories offer explicit claims for their universal applicability on the basis that they have identified the fundamental organising principles of human society. Thus Marxism builds its theory of the development of all human societies across time on the universality of human needs, the simple fact that everyone needs food and shelter, whereas sociobiology seeks to explain all human behaviour in terms of biological imperatives, given that human biology has scarcely changed in thousands of years. The more ambitious a theory, the more aspects of human life it attempts to explain – and especially if it claims to be valid for all human societies at all periods – then the more likely it is that it will be accused of being simplistic, of ignoring the complexities of human behaviour and historical development, of reducing everything to a single determining factor. Those who reject such theories do not deny that, for example, material needs and inherited instincts do affect some areas of human behaviour; it is a question of how much weight is placed on such 'universal factors', and how much they are expected to explain. On the other hand, the more that a theory is reduced in scope, the less explanatory power it has, and the less possibility it offers of making comparisons between periods.

These issues can be illustrated from the history of theories of urbanism and its effects. In the mid-twentieth century, cities were often positively identified with economic development, both in early modern European history and in the contemporary Third World: they were indicators of the level of economic progress, 'electric transformers', 'accelerators of all historical time'.[18] At the same period, the Chicago School of urban sociology argued that their observations of aspects of contemporary American urban life – including alienation, individualism and fragmented, even 'schizophrenic', social relationships – were universal features of 'urbanism', the consequences of living in large cities.[19] In neither case was the concept of 'city' clearly defined; it was taken to be self-evident, a matter of common sense, something that could be found in all historical societies. The obvious objection to these theories was to put forward examples of cities, both historical and contemporary, that did not seem to have a positive influence on the economies of their hinterlands and with societies that exhibited striking differences from modern Chicago. Historians and sociologists therefore reduced the breadth of their generalisations by turning to approaches that emphasised historical and regional variation, reviving the tradition of developing typologies of cities: industrial and pre-industrial, generative and parasitic,

European and Oriental. Only some cities – those of early modern Europe and the modern West, above all – were now characterised as progressive. Third World cities that lacked dynamic relationships with their hinterlands no longer contradicted the theory but could be explained in its terms: they were not progressive because they did not conform to the Western model of cities.

This is the tradition within which Finley's work is located: following German sociologists of the turn of the century such as Sombart and Weber, he distinguishes the ancient city from the medieval, as consumer rather than producer, and thus characterises it as an impediment to economic development rather than as a stimulus.[20] It is notable that he chooses to generalise about the 'ancient' city rather than the 'Greek' or 'Roman' city; he justifies this on the basis of the shared cultural attitudes to urbanism that he detects in Greek and Roman sources (which is, however, clearly distinguished from modern 'urbanism'), and on the grounds that they share the same basic relationship between city and hinterland. Most subsequent studies of ancient urbanism have focused on either Greek or Roman cities; partly this reflects the fact that most historians specialise in one period or the other, but it is also the case that many historians detect significant differences between Greek and Roman cities, and even between cities in different regions (under the Roman Empire, for example, the long-established cities of Italy or Asia Minor compared with the foundations in Gaul or Britain).[21] It is a question of judgement: do the similarities between ancient cities of different periods and regions (especially when contrasted with other, quite distinct, city types such as the medieval and the modern) outweigh the equally obvious differences, or should Finley's broad model be abandoned in favour of something more historically specific (but hence less powerful)?

Either approach has to assume that that there is indeed such a thing as a 'city', of which Greek, Roman, medieval, Oriental and modern cities are variants – even if it has proved impossible to produce a definition that actually works for all historical periods. Greek and Roman writers themselves struggled over the question of whether a 'city' should be defined by its size, by its political institutions or by its facilities; modern urban sociologists have faced the same problem.[22] The majority of places identified as cities in antiquity would not be counted as such according to the criteria used to distinguish 'towns' from 'cities' in the early modern period, let alone the modern.

It will not have escaped notice that I have so far avoided defining what I mean by a city. Neither geographers nor sociologists nor historians have succeeded in agreeing on a definition. Yet we all know sufficiently what we mean by the label, in general terms ... The block in definition arises from the difficulties, apparently insuperable, of incorporating all the essential variables without excluding whole periods of history in which we all know cities existed, and on the other hand, of settling for a least common denominator without lodging on a level of generality that serves no useful purpose.[23]

It is difficult to see how such vagueness can be accepted, if 'the city' is then going to be assigned a key role as either stimulus or impediment to economic development. 'We all know sufficiently what we mean by the label, in general terms': this seems to invite the projection into the past of our own assumptions about cities, built up from a mixture of experience and cultural baggage – including the long-standing association of cities with modernity.[24] Some sociologists have argued that theories of urbanism are examples of the 'fallacy of misplaced concreteness', in which symptoms of changes in society as a whole – increased division of labour, say, or the more impersonal, segmented social relationships associated with modernity – are ascribed to the city as an agent, rather than the city as the place where they tend to be most visible.[25] Certainly, if we cannot agree on a general, transhistorical definition of what constitutes a city, it is difficult to see how we can make use of broad generalisations about the effects of urbanism in studying cities in the ancient world.[26]

Laws, models and types

The second aspect of any generalisation that needs to be considered and evaluated might be termed its 'strength' or its 'status'. What sort of knowledge does it claim to provide – a definitive statement about how the world works, an idea of how the world might work in ideal circumstances, or an observation of how the world often tends to work? This affects the usefulness of the theory – a 'strong' generalisation, if accepted, tells you how things *must* have been, rather than simply how they might have been – but also its plausibility. The stronger the claim, the more likely it is that the theory will have to account for evidence and examples that appear to be incompatible with its assertions.

The strongest form of generalisation may be termed a law: a statement of how particular phenomena will always behave. A number of
writers in the nineteenth century sought the historical equivalent of
Newtonian physics, a set of laws governing the behaviour of human
beings that would have the same explanatory and predictive power
for society as physics and chemistry had apparently provided for
the natural world. Marxism, which developed within this tradition,
retains something of this perspective in its search for the 'laws of
motion' of capitalism: society is imagined as a complex machine, the
inner workings of which may be exposed, revealing the inherent tendency of the modern social order to bring about its own downfall. It
should be noted that, while Marx frequently refers to his search for
the 'laws' that shaped human behaviour whether or not individuals
were aware of them, he was equally interested in the ways that humans were able to alter the world around them, including the 'laws'
that affected their behaviour. 'Men make their own history, but they
do not make it just as they please'; this is not quite a contradiction,
but certainly an inconsistency.[27] Few contemporary Marxists believe
that the replacement of capitalism by communism is an inevitable
historical process, or that these 'laws of motion' are really analogous
to scientific laws.[28] Nevertheless, most attacks on Marxism focus on
the idea that it claims to have identified the hidden determinants
of human behaviour and the underlying principles of historical development: not only are these generalisations felt to be excessively
broad and simplistic, they are deterministic (denying, or at least
limiting, human choice and free will), teleological (ignoring the role
of contingency and chance in history) and, of course, politically dubious.[29] Other attempts at formulating explicit historical and social
laws may be criticised on the same grounds: for example, the theory
of Oswald Spengler that civilisations are, like biological organisms,
subject to predictable cycles of growth, maturity, decay and death,
and hence, on the basis of the test case of the Roman Empire, our
own civilisation has embarked on an inevitable decline.[30]

The nineteenth-century positivistic conception of a 'law' as a definitive statement of how the real world actually works is in fact out
of step with current thinking on the nature of scientific knowledge.[31]
Scientific theories are now seen not as absolute truths but as working hypotheses, which for the moment fit the evidence better than
alternative theories but are always liable to being replaced (just as
Newtonian physics was superseded by relativity; note that Newton's
laws still work in most situations). Epistemologically, they have a

similar status to historical interpretations, although the evidence underpinning them is generally of higher quality, as scientists are able to gather experimental data under controlled conditions. However, this does not mean that historians no longer need concern themselves with the idea of absolute scientific or pseudo-scientific laws. In the first place, many scientists retain a positivistic outlook in their work, regardless of what the philosophers of science might say, and hence, for example, the hypothesis that the behaviour of individuals and groups is determined not by conscious thought but by the drive of the gene to reproduce itself may be presented as scientific fact rather than theory.[32] The same is true of some social scientists, notably economists, despite their dismal record in actually predicting the future behaviour of the world economy. Second, historians are not always clear about the status of their generalisations, so that they may present a hypothesis as a universal law ('city air makes men free'; 'cities are electric transformers'), or simply assume the universal validity of their assumptions about 'human nature'.

In theory, such 'laws', explicit or implicit, should be easy to evaluate: they cannot ever be proved correct, however much supporting evidence is accumulated (though obviously that adds to their plausibility), but they can be proved wrong ('falsified') by a single contrary example.[33] This provides grounds for reducing their scope ('not valid for all societies') or qualifying their claims ('not valid in all circumstances') or rejecting them altogether. In practice, this is not so straightforward. The alleged law may be so vaguely formulated that it is impossible to falsify – in which case it is hardly likely to be very useful, or to have inspired a particularly productive analysis. It is often sufficient simply to highlight the assumptions underpinning an interpretation to force a re-evaluation (for example, pointing out, as discussed above, that Finley and other urban theorists simply assume that there is a universal social object called a 'city' that always acts in some way on the society around it).

Not all theories are so vulnerable to criticism: given certain basic assumptions, they are internally consistent and impossible to falsify. Historical evidence is not made up of pre-existing, objective facts; it is produced through a process of interpretation, and so it can always be reinterpreted in line with a particular theory – or simply explained away. More than one internally coherent theory may therefore fit the known 'facts' (a situation known as underdetermination). This is even more of a problem when direct evidence does not exist. When examining questions of cause and effect, we cannot run controlled experiments to isolate determining factors from incidentals; historical causation always remains a matter of debate. We can study patterns of human behaviour, but we cannot directly study what motivates that behaviour, or determine whether it is due to inherited instincts, repressed desires or conscious rationality. In practice, most historians instinctively reject monocausal and reductive laws of history because they find them simplistic and unconvincing, rather than because they have been proved definitively wrong. A good interpretation should be able to account for as much of the existing evidence as possible without having to explain away too much, and it should be compatible with the rest of our knowledge of the world – or produce convincing arguments to persuade us to abandon the assumptions about free will and determinism that lead us to reject the idea of grand historical and social laws.

Most of the theories that have been adopted by historians make less grandiose claims and take a more sophisticated approach to understanding human behaviour. Rather than offering absolute laws, they generate claims to the effect that X is true in particular circumstances and therefore may be true, or at least may be a significant factor, in similar situations. At a basic level, this may simply involve the use of comparative evidence from other historical periods; thus one might draw on a study of the impact of London on the economy of sixteenth-century England as a source of ideas for considering the impact of ancient Rome on the rest of Italy, on the basis that they were both large 'metropolitan' cities in pre-industrial economies, which needed to draw supplies from a large area.[34] The most useful theories, however, are less closely tied to specific historical situations and hence, potentially, more widely applicable. They acknowledge that reality is complex, and that historical and social processes have multiple inter-related causes, but they argue that it is possible to identify underlying regularities, and to distinguish between more and less important causative factors, by making use of simplified, abstract approximations of reality: models.

In social scientific terms, a model is 'an intellectual construct which simplifies reality in order to emphasise the recurrent, the constant and the typical.'[35] An alternative characterisation is as:

> a simplified structuring of reality which presents supposedly significant relationships in a generalized form. Models are highly subjective approximations in that they do not include all

associated observations or measurements, but as such they are valuable in obscuring incidental detail and in allowing fundamental aspects of reality to appear. This selectivity means that models have varying degrees of probability and a limited range of conditions over which they apply.[36]

In other words, whereas historians tend to criticise theories and laws for excessive simplification of a complex historical reality, here the simplification is deliberate, an essential step in the intellectual process. This can be illustrated by looking at three different ways in which models may be employed to develop our understanding of human society.

First, an artificially simplified model of reality may be constructed as a means of identifying and exploring causal relationships. This is, in a sense, a kind of thought experiment analogous to a scientific experiment, in so far as it aims to reduce the number of variables involved in a process to highlight how particular factors interact. The most obvious examples of this approach are economic theories. Many of these are derived not from empirical data about the functioning of markets but from abstract models of markets, often mathematical, in which it is assumed that all participants are economically rational (that is, they will always seek to maximise utility) and have perfect, costless information about costs, prices, and so forth. These are assumptions that never hold true in reality; but, by excluding motivation and knowledge as variables, economists are able to study the interaction of the other variables (supply and demand, interest rates, returns on investment, and so forth). This produces general statements about economic processes that hold true in particular circumstances, namely the artificially simplified world of the model.

A classic example of this intellectual technique is the 'Isolated State' model developed by J.H. von Thünen in the early nineteenth century as a means of investigating the effects of changing production costs on agricultural practices:

> Imagine a very large town, at the centre of a fertile plain which is crossed by no navigable river or canal. Throughout the plain the soil is capable of cultivation and of the same fertility. Far from the town, the plain turns into an uncultivated wilderness which cuts off all communication between this state and the outside world ... The problem we want to solve is this: What

pattern of cultivation will take shape in these conditions?; and how will the farming system of the different districts be affected by their distance from the town. We assume throughout that farming is conducted absolutely rationally.[37]

Different crops, von Thünen argues, have different rent–distance functions; that is, the economic rent (net value of returns on production) they yield alters with distance from the central market, as the cost of land decreases and the cost of transport increases. At a given distance from the city, therefore, it is economically rational to grow one crop rather than another. The result is a pattern, now familiar from elementary geography, of concentric zones of production around the urban centre, each one featuring a different crop type and a different degree of intensity of cultivation.

In devising this model, von Thünen drew on experience and empirical evidence, but its assumptions about uniform fertility, uniform transport costs, complete isolation and perfect economic rationality are clearly unrealistic. The point is that, having identified the way that rent–distance functions operate in idealised conditions, we can then compare this with the empirical evidence for production strategies in a given region. For example, it offers a plausible explanation for the fact that Kent in the sixteenth century became a centre of market gardening supplying the London market. We can then investigate land-use patterns in the *suburbium* around ancient Rome, not just with the idea that they might resemble the situation around early modern London but with a proper understanding of the economic principles that chiefly determined what happened around London. If the predictions of the theory are completely at odds with the empirical evidence, we need to rethink the model; either it is logically flawed, or its assumptions are simply too unrealistic. We do not expect that reality *ought* to conform to the model (although admittedly some economists do seem to proceed on this basis in developing policy proposals). Indeed, divergences from the model may be interesting in themselves, revealing something of the range of different factors that might influence decisions about land use – as seen in the Roman *suburbium*, which is revealed as the site of fierce competition for land and water between agricultural producers, the wealthy elite seeking to construct luxury villas and parks, and the demands of the city for somewhere to bury its dead.

In a way, this sort of model offers another form of comparative evidence, a comparison not between different historical periods but between reality and a simplified intellectual construct of reality. As with historical comparisons, we need to consider whether the comparison is appropriate; whether the differences between the two situations (in this case, the wholly unrealistic assumptions of the model) are likely to be less significant than the logical consistency and (arguably) universal validity of the economic principle. There is then a further move involved in extending a model developed to understand modern economic practices to an earlier historical period; for example, von Thünen assumes that agriculture is market oriented, so we would not expect his theory to apply to a society based on subsistence-oriented peasant smallholdings. Of course, if we then find the same patterns of land use around an urban centre in such a society, this raises questions about the assumption that peasant agriculture is not influenced by the demands of the market. The basic question is whether the economic principles identified in the controlled circumstances of the model offer a plausible explanation of behaviour observed in the real world.

As has already been discussed, it is a common criticism of the application of modern economic theory to ancient history that it simply assumes the existence of a form of behaviour ('economic rationality') found only occasionally in the modern West – and, apparently, found mainly among economists rather than the population as a whole. In fact this is a problem not of the economic theory, which could scarcely have been developed without making use of simplifying assumptions of this kind, but of the way in which the theory is then applied to actual situations. It is problematic to assume that economic rationality is a universal human trait and thus that economic theory *must* always apply; economics does not produce laws of human behaviour but theories of how factors interact in an idealised situation which resembles (arguably) but does not conform to reality. It is equally problematic to assume that, because an economic principle was developed on the basis of an idealised model, it can never have any validity for the ancient world. Of course, we may reject the theory because the model's assumptions are, according to our own assumptions, completely untenable; thus Marxism criticises conventional economics on the grounds that it describes human behaviour under capitalism rather than human behaviour in general. We may criticise the internal logic and consistency of the model or reject it because it offers a less persuasive or less useful interpretation of the evidence than another approach. However, to reject it for making simplifying assumptions as a means of identifying underlying principles misses the point.

The second approach to model building is to use empirical evidence to produce an idealised construct of an institution or a process, identifying essential attributes, regularities and recurrent features. Such general concepts as 'pre-industrial', 'family', 'state' and 'city' are models of this type, derived from a range of actual cases that clearly differ from one another but are felt to have enough in common to support the notion that they are examples of a more general type. Such models may be 'monothetic', identifying the essential feature(s) which all examples of the type must possess (as, for example, most definitions would agree that a 'city' has to have a large population – relative to its historical context – concentrated in a relatively small area), or 'polythetic', identifying a range of features of which examples of the type will possess most but not necessarily all (thus a 'city' may be a religious centre, a political, economic or cultural centre, but not necessarily all of them together, while a religious centre such as a monastery or a shrine is not necessarily a city).

Historians make use of such general concepts all the time, without necessarily being clear about their logical status. They debate regularly about whether a particular case should be classified as an example of a particular concept: was republican Rome 'democratic'; was the Delian League an 'empire'? This is because such concepts are not simply a convenient means of classification, of simplifying reality, though of course they serve that purpose well. Rather, membership of the group is taken to carry implications about the nature of the particular case, how it relates to wider society and how it should be studied. Thus, as we have seen, it has often been assumed that something identified as a 'city' will have a positive effect on economic development. Studying the Delian League as an 'empire', comparable with other empires, raises all sorts of interesting research questions and opens up the possibility of drawing on ideas from other periods and disciplines. However, it is important to be conscious of the status of the argument; the Delian League is not intrinsically an empire, and therefore it is not bound by any supposed 'laws' of empire. Rather, it may be *thought of* as an empire; it resembles an abstract model of 'empire' in some respects, and therefore it may resemble it in others. On the other hand, there may be grounds for arguing that its differences from other empires are more significant than its resemblances, in which case we would not expect to learn anything from the comparison. What matters is whether or not the model offers a more persuasive interpretation of the evidence than alternative approaches. Certainly we need to be conscious of the fact that we are dealing with intellectual constructs, ways of thinking, not real objects, and we need to be wary of the baggage of unconscious assumptions that such general concepts as 'empire' and 'city' tend to bring with them.

Finley's 'consumer city' is a particular sort of model, an 'ideal type', following the approach developed by the German sociologist Max Weber:

> An ideal type is achieved by the one-sided *accentuation* of one or more points of view and by the synthesis of many diffuse, discrete, more or less present and occasionally absent *individual* phenomena, which are arranged according to those one-sidedly emphasized viewpoints into a unified mental construct. In its conceptual purity, this mental construct can never be found empirically in reality. It is a *utopia*. *Historical* research faces the task of determining in each *individual* case, the extent to which this ideal-construct approximates to or diverges from reality.[38]

The important point about Weberian ideal types is that they do not usually occur singly; rather, one type is defined in contrast to other types, as the 'consumer city' is distinguished from the 'producer city'. The model is intended to highlight what ancient cities have in common that distinguishes them from medieval cities, and hence it gives them a different role in relation to economic development.

In theory, the relationship between model and evidence is always two way. 'It is in the nature of models that they are subject to constant adjustment, correction, modification or outright replacement.'[39] The ideal type is based on historical evidence; it then offers a way of interpreting the evidence; in turn, the evidence should be used to produce a more refined model that better matches reality. In practice, because the evidence is always open to interpretation, the model tends to become fixed, the point around which the arguments revolve. Certainly this became the case with the 'consumer city' hypothesis. It is fair to say that, on the whole, ancient cities resemble the 'consumer' ideal type more than they do the 'producer'; that is not to say that this is the only or even the best way of characterising Greek or Roman cities, let alone that we have to accept the assumption of Finley and Weber that 'consumer' cities always have a negative influence on economic development. However, the argument among ancient historians tended to get stuck at the earlier stage of whether or not the ancient city really was a consumer.

This was really the wrong argument to pursue, and this wrong turn explains why so many historians now feel that the debate about the nature of the ancient city has reached a dead end.[40] The 'consumer city' model proved more or less impossible to pin down and refute, for a number of reasons. We have no direct evidence about the economic relationship between town and countryside, and the evidence we do have for town–country exchange, urban manufacturing, and so forth can be interpreted in such a way as to fit either the consumer or the non-consumer model. The ideal type is polythetic, based on several different attributes rather than a single defining feature, so that it cannot be disproved by demonstrating that one of these attributes does not hold true in a particular case; showing that the city could be a centre of trade and industry, as many historians attempted to do, does nothing to lessen the contrast with the medieval city in political and social terms and so does not disprove the model. Finally, the notion of the 'typical' ancient city becomes problematic if this means that too much contrary evidence can be explained away as coming from 'non-typical' cities – which at times seems to include any city about which we actually know anything.

> The model of a 'consumer city' and indeed the whole analysis I have attempted of the ancient economy would not be in the least affected or impaired by the discovery of a few more textile workshops in Pompeii or a few more members of the senatorial aristocracy who actively engaged in commerce and manufacture. There can be no dispute over the existence of exceptional men, even of exceptional cities. No historical or sociological model pretends to incorporate all known or possible instances. In the absence of meaningful quantitative data, the best that one can do is judge whether or not a model, a set of concepts, explains the available data more satisfactorily than a competing model.[41]

Ideal types can seem frustratingly elusive if one forgets – as Finley did not – that they are simply models; they cannot be proved or disproved but simply judged more or less persuasive and productive. The proper question is not whether the typical ancient city was a consumer but whether thinking about ancient cities in terms of the consumer city model and its implications tells us anything useful. Models are tools, not ends in themselves; if they fail to account for the evidence persuasively, if they seem to rest on dubious assumptions, or, most importantly, if they fail to suggest interesting new ways of thinking about the past, then they need to be replaced.

The same can be said of the third form of model building, that of constructing abstract models of structures and processes within a given society. The aim here is not to generalise for the purposes of comparison with other societies, but to provide a template for understanding complex social and economic processes. Much as a map of the London Underground does not attempt to provide an accurate representation of what is actually on the ground but aims to show, as clearly as possible, the relationships between different stations, so the model offers a deliberately abstract and schematic representation of the relationships between different factors. 'It is meant, rather like a passport photo or a menu, only as a guide to a complex reality, not as a replacement for it.'[42] Two of the most striking examples of such model building in the field of ancient history can be found in the work of Keith Hopkins: the 'taxes and trade' model, covering the economic impact of Roman imperialism, and the model in his book *Conquerors and Slaves* of the impact of Roman conquests on the economy and society of Italy.[43]

Both models aim at highlighting processes that had far-reaching effects on the economy and society of the Roman Empire but of which the Romans were almost completely unaware; hindsight, and more sophisticated analytical tools, give us an enormous advantage in understanding. The models are constructed in the same manner, incorporating three different layers of argument. At the bottom is the ancient evidence. Hopkins emphasises deduction rather than induction as his intellectual approach; he begins with general concepts and uses these to interpret the evidence, rather than expecting the evidence to 'speak' to him. Moreover, he is candid about its limitations, and the limitations of conventional historiography:

> It is not possible to prove this assertion by the traditional method of selective quotation from classical sources ... My assertion is compatible with such passages in the sources, but cannot be validated by them. Instead, I have tried to consider both the probability and the consequences of the assertion being wrong, and then to ask: What alternative assertion is more likely to be true?[44]

However, the evidence remains important in two respects: it can illustrate, if not prove, his more general hypotheses (for example, taking a graph of shipwrecks in the Mediterranean as an indication of an increase in the volume of trade under the Roman Empire) and it serves to test them, as his theory's claim to truth is based on its being able to account for the evidence better than any alternative theory.

The second level of each model is a series of propositions, most of which are admitted to be unprovable: 'It is difficult to prove that each proposition is right . . . the generalisations advanced are disproportionately large in relation to the surrounding evidence.'[45] Some are presented on the basis of their logical consistency and economy, others on the basis that they reflect known economic principles (for example, the relation between money supply and prices). Most strikingly, they are presented as backing one another up in what he characterises as the wigwam argument: 'each pole would fall down by itself, but together the poles stand up, by leaning on each other; they point roughly in the same direction, and circumscribe truth.'[46] That is to say, a series of plausible but unprovable hypotheses, when taken together, amount to a more persuasive argument. This is the third level of the model, the overall conception or schema, which shows how the various factors are inter-related, revealing how the levying of taxes in conquered provinces led to an increase in economic activity through the Empire, and how the rewards and costs of Rome's military adventures brought about the dispossession of the Italian peasantry and the growth of the city of Rome. The models seek to do justice to the complexity of historical change: it is not presented as a simple process of cause and effect but as a series of mutually influencing factors and feedback loops, which in the case of *Conquerors and Slaves* are presented in the unusual (for ancient history, at least) form of a flow diagram.

Like other models, Hopkins's theories offer templates for thinking about the ancient world, overarching frameworks that suggest new ways of interpreting the evidence and new lines of enquiry. They differ from other such interpretative constructs in the explicitness with which he develops his arguments and signposts his guiding assumptions and intellectual strategies; in evaluating other models, we are made to do more of the work ourselves. Hopkins argues that, given the limitations of the ancient evidence, all historians can ever do is produce competing fictions about the past and try to judge their plausibility; he is simply more open about the logical status of his arguments and the basis on which he judges the plausibility of interpretations (namely, compatibility with what economics and sociology tell us about the workings of human society). Most of the criticism of his models has focused at level of evidence, arguing, for example, that Roman taxes were often collected in kind rather than cash as the model assumes, thus implicitly rejecting both his methodology and his overall aims, since no attempt is made at offering an alternative model of the internal mechanisms of the Empire. It remains in part a matter of taste: what sort of knowledge do we want of the past, a grand explanatory framework or isolated pieces of information? If we wish to understand the complex ways in which different parts of ancient society interacted, Hopkins's work suggests that carefully formulated abstract models are indispensable.

Vocabulary

Hopkins's substantive theories about the workings of the Roman Empire have been extensively debated, but his model-building approach has not been widely imitated. In part this must reflect the usual suspicion of generalisations that try to explain too much, especially when presented with such a cavalier attitude towards the ancient evidence; this is not the sort of knowledge of antiquity that most historians desire. But it is also the case that Hopkins's articles *appear* off-putting and alien: he not only makes a case for abandoning many of the traditional practices of historiography but enacts it through the form in which he presents his arguments, deploying explicit propositional statements, technical social-scientific terminology, economic formulae and flow diagrams. This is not how ancient history is traditionally written.

The use of technical vocabulary – commonly disparaged as 'jargon' – is an important feature of many theoretical approaches to history; it is certainly the most immediately obvious, and indeed one might suspect that many works are identified as 'theoretical' on the basis not so much of their methodology or aims as of their rhetoric, in contrast to conventional history's reliance on 'everyday' language. Technical language – it is only 'jargon' when someone else uses it – has a number of functions. It aims at achieving a greater degree of precision in describing complex and unfamiliar objects and processes – particularly if, as is often the case, a term has no equivalent in 'everyday' language. It emphasises the possibility of making cross-cultural comparisons, highlighting the resemblance of a particular instance to a more general model, whereas describing objects in terms specific to a particular historical society implies that they are not comparable to anything else. Third, it operates as a form of shorthand, an aid to communication; the term 'consumer city' can be deployed in a historical argument without necessarily requiring further elaboration, on the basis that other historians will be familiar with the term and arguments and assumptions that lie behind it.

However, the use of technical language does raise two issues of concern for the majority of ancient historians. First, there is the question of anachronism, of whether describing antiquity in terms developed to understand the modern world is inevitably misleading because it distorts the evidence, ignoring the particularity of the past and suppressing key differences between past and present. As one proponent of this argument put it, 'I have not contaminated the presentation of the evidence from the Roman empire with conceptions drawn from wider sociological studies.'[47] Taken to its logical conclusion, this implies that the only appropriate way of describing antiquity is in ancient terms, since all of our modern words have anachronistic connotations. In practice, of course, historians are happy to use a word such as 'city', although it has rather different overtones and associations from such ancient terms as *polis, astu, municipium* and *urbs*; indeed, it is only by 'translating' ancient concepts into our anachronistic vocabulary that we can develop any sort of understanding of the past. Of course modern terms may be misleading, but there is no logical reason why social-scientific terminology should be *more* misleading than everyday language; indeed, it can be argued that it is less likely to mislead, because it is more obvious that it carries modern overtones (whereas one might pass over a phrase such as 'the Roman middle class' without registering the possible anachronism) and because those who deploy such terminology are generally more explicit and self-conscious about their choice of language.

We do not have the option of a neutral, transparent, 'normal' language; we simply have to choose from a range of possible vocabularies, some more precise and technical than others but all equally time-bound and laden with anachronistic baggage. The past can always be redescribed in different ways; it is a question of what vocabulary is felt to be appropriate for describing a particular aspect of the past, and that may be determined by our assumptions about what the past was like.

The materials and means of labour, a proportion of which consists of the products of previous work, play their part in every labour process in every age and in all circumstances. If, therefore, I label them 'capital' in the confident knowledge that 'semper aliquid haeret' ['something always sticks'], then I have proved that the existence of capital is an eternal law of nature of human production and that the Xinghiz who cuts down rushes with a knife he has stolen from a Russian so as to weave them together to make a canoe is just as true a capitalist as Herr von Rothschild. I could prove with equal facility that the Greeks and Romans celebrated communion because they drank wine and ate bread.[48]

Marx would concede that this behaviour *could* be described as capitalist; his point is that this is not a neutral description but a concealed argument, positing the universality of values and motives associated with the modern West. According to his view of pre-modern economies, there is a more appropriate vocabulary for analysing such situations; for someone of opposing views, of course, it is the Marxist vocabulary of 'modes of production' and the like that will seem anachronistic and misleading. This is rightly a matter of debate (albeit a debate that is never likely to be resolved); what is not acceptable is the idea that there is a problem with only certain sorts of language, that if one simply avoids terminology derived from the social sciences there is no need to consider the effects or implications of one's choice of words.

The second area of concern about social-scientific terminology is that, at the same time as it eases communication among those who share the same assumptions and theoretical background, it renders the account less accessible to anyone else. There is some truth in this suggestion, just as the use of words such as *polis* or *equites* in ancient history exclude non-specialists. In either case, these are felt to be the most useful and appropriate words for describing the past; the reader is expected to make a certain amount of effort to get to grips with the technical vocabulary, rather than the historian having to spell everything out. There is always a need to balance precision and accessibility in any area of ancient history. It is not generally true, whatever traditionalists might feel, that technical language is used deliberately to exclude everyone who is not part of the group of theoretical initiates; but social-scientific vocabulary certainly can be deployed rhetorically to establish the historian as a particular kind of authority, offering a particular sort of account of the past.[49]

A more serious problem in communication may arise when a term is not immediately identifiable as a technical one, because it also has a meaning in 'ordinary' language. Some common theoretical concepts were originally adopted from everyday speech and acquired a more specialised meaning from their use in theoretical discussions: class, capitalism, labour, society.[50] Others were originally devised in the context of a particular theory, with very specific technical meanings, but have been absorbed into the wider vernacular in a watered-down and occasionally garbled form: this is the case, for example, with much of the vocabulary of Freudian psychoanalysis, such as 'repression'. Words constantly change their meanings over time, especially 'key' words, which play a central place in particular debates, and they constantly acquire wider connotations and associations.

> Present-day overtones of the word 'consumer' should not be allowed to intrude and mislead. No one is suggesting that the urban lower classes were a host of beggars and pensioners, though it has become a favourite scholarly pastime to 'disprove' that contention for the city of Rome ... The issue implicit in the notion of the consumer-city is whether and how far the economy and the power relations within the town rested on wealth generated by rents and taxes flowing to, and circulating among, town-dwellers. Even the quintessential consumer-city, Rome, required innumerable craftsmen and shopkeepers for intra-urban production and circulation. In so far as they were engaged in 'petty commodity production', the production by independent craftsmen of goods retailed for local consumption, they do no invalidate the notion of a consumer-city.[51]

On the one hand, the label 'consumer city' gives a neat indication of the essence of the model, whereas an original term with no particular associations – the 'Type A city', perhaps, or the *esthiopolis* – might be rather less effective or memorable. On the other hand, some of the other associations of the word 'consumer' create the possibility of confusion, making the model appear to claim things that are in fact not part of its argument, such as the notion (familiar from Juvenal's line about bread and circuses) that all ancient city dwellers were idle parasites.

Often, the major contribution of a theory, and the reason why it is felt to be a productive way of studying some aspect of society, is the creation of a new vocabulary and hence a new way of thinking about the world. Naming something that has not previously been named does in a sense bring it into existence. For example, in retrospect 'patriarchy' (male subordination of women) is seen to have been the dominant form of social organisation in Europe and the rest of the world for millennia; but only when it was named as such, rather than simply assumed to be the natural order of society, could it be properly analysed and criticised. Sometimes this intellectual development involves strange and unfamiliar words; sometimes it involves the reinterpretation and appropriation of existing words, which can be equally disconcerting. In any case, historians need to be fully conscious and critical of their own and others' use of language. Words can mislead readers, if not writers, through unintended associations and overtones. They can also reveal a historian's theoretical assumptions (thus 'class', 'alienation' and 'mode of production' tend to indicate Marxism, whereas 'marginal utility' and 'diminishing returns' point to neoclassical economics), while an essential strategy in evaluating any historical interpretation is to identify the key terms, the concepts that are being made to do a lot of work in the argument.

Conclusion

The first step in evaluating a theoretical approach to history is to realise that it is there; some historians make their assumptions and methodology explicit, but in many cases key generalisations are left hidden, perhaps even from the historians themselves. Most historical accounts focus on the interpretation of individual pieces of evidence, rather than on the wider framework of ideas that govern their interpretations; when evaluating them, we need to consider both. A good theory needs to be internally coherent and economical to fit with the evidence – and to fit with what else we know about the world, including principles and models derived from the social sciences.

For example, Finley's consumer city model has been attacked on the grounds that cities such as Pompeii show evidence of significant trade and industry and hence should not be characterised as mere 'consumers'; that the model takes the value-laden statements of members of the elite about proper economic behaviour at face value, and assumes that they apply to the whole of ancient society rather than just to the elite; that it ignores significant differences between Greek and Roman cities, and works less well for the Roman period; that it offers a reasonable description of the ancient city but that the implications of this for ancient economic development are quite different from what Finley assumes; and finally, that Finley's overall view of the ancient economy is discredited by its association with the anti-Western ideas of the Khmer Rouge and the Sendero Luminoso. With the exception of the last, these are all valid arguments, operating at different levels – and there are responses to each of them. Neither the ancient evidence nor modern social-scientific principles are ultimately decisive. In the end, it is a matter of choosing between plausible interpretations on the basis of our own assumptions.

The final test of any theory is not just whether it is persuasive but whether it is productive, offering new ways of thinking about the ancient world. Most historical theories end up being abandoned not because they have been proved wrong but simply because they have ceased to raise interesting questions or suggest new lines of research – a fate that now seems likely to overtake the 'consumer city' model. Of course, it can also be productive to return to an old theory with a new perspective – which is precisely what Finley did, rereading the works of Weber and others on the ancient city – while some venerable theories continue to stimulate at least some historians. The aim of the rest of this book is to introduce a range of theories that have led ancient historians to view the past in a different light. Part of the argument of this chapter has been that some sort of theory, however vague and unsystematic, is indispensable; as Finley put it, 'without one . . . there can be no explanation; there can only be reportage and crude taxonomy, antiquarianism in its narrowest sense'.[52] The positive argument is that, while 'theory' can be disconcerting, frustrating and even aggravating, it can also be inspiring.

Chapter 2

Ancient and modern

The invention of the ancient economy

> The literature of the ancients, their legislation, their public treaties, and their administration of the conquered provinces, all proclaim their utter ignorance of the nature and origin of wealth, of the manner in which it is distributed, and of the effects of its consumption.[1]

If ancient historians wish to avoid distorting their evidence by imposing anachronistic modern concepts on it, they must stay off the topic of 'the ancient economy' altogether. The words 'economy' and 'economics' are derived from the Greek *oikonomia*, meaning 'household management', but the concepts they embody are wholly modern. The idea that trade, agriculture, industry, money-lending and other such activities should be thought of as different facets of a single activity known as 'production' might perhaps be comprehensible, if not acceptable, to Greek or Roman writers, who devoted some thought to drawing clear distinctions between different forms of 'acquisition' on social and moral grounds (agriculture was for gentlemen, handiwork and retail were for the unwashed masses). Such activities might be discussed under the heading of *oikonomia* in so far as they formed part of the duties of the head of the household – but the proper conduct of marital relations and behaviour towards one's slaves came under the same heading. Ancient writers occasionally talked about the *oikonomia* of the city, suggesting that civic leaders should think of themselves as heads of families managing their household's income and expenditure. However, the idea that a city, a region or a nation might possess such a thing as an 'economy', which needed to be monitored, managed, studied and stimulated, and which determined the fortunes of its inhabitants, was an invention of the late eighteenth century. As Finley noted in his classic work *The Ancient Economy*:

of course they farmed, traded, manufactured, mined, taxed, coined, deposited and loaned money, made profits or failed in their enterprises. And they discussed these activities in their talk and their writing. What they did not do, however, was to combine these particular activities conceptually into a unit.[2]

Modern studies of ancient economic activity have to operate under two important constraints. First, the evidence is patchy, limited in quantity and often only tangentially relevant to the subject. Having failed to develop an 'economic' perspective on the world, Greek and Roman writers had no particular reason to collect or discuss material relating to such activities, while ancient states never collected the vast quantities of statistical data on revenues, taxes, national wealth and the like that characterise later periods. As one eminent ancient economic historian put it, 'it is unlikely that I shall long be able to conceal the ignominious truth, that there are no ancient statistics'.[3] Second, and more significantly, there is a methodological problem. Historians cannot avoid using at least some 'anachronistic' concepts, since it is only because they are organising their research around the modern category of 'economic activity' that they would consider bringing together such diverse pieces of evidence as the letters of Pliny, the archaeology of Roman shipwrecks and Cicero's *De Officiis*, or Aristophanes' *Acharnians* and the speeches of Lysias. The question is rather *which* modern conceptual framework should be brought to bear, choosing from the range of different theories about the relation between 'the economy' and the rest of society that the modern world has to offer. This choice is closely related to the way in which we conceive of the relation between past and present, the balance between the 'sameness' and 'difference' of antiquity. In other words, 'theory' of some kind is indispensable in ancient economic history.

The eighteenth- and nineteenth-century inventors of the concept of 'the economy', and of the science that was intended to reveal its workings and advise politicians on how to manage it, were well aware of their own originality. The writings of Plato and Aristotle might continue to dominate the study of philosophy and politics, but Adam Smith, Thomas Malthus and their followers took pride in the fact that they had developed an entirely new – and, in their view, more powerful – way of understanding human society. This also offered the possibility of understanding classical antiquity better than the Greeks or Romans did themselves, by revealing the sources of the wealth that supported the creation of 'classical civilisation'. The early political economists assumed that the economic organisation of the ancient world was not significantly different from their own, at least in part because they had not realised the full significance of the Industrial Revolution that was taking place around them. Greece and Rome were wealthy, sophisticated societies, founded on agriculture but with extensive trade and a high level of culture; this was essentially how they regarded their own society, except that the modern world had the intellectual advantage of understanding the sources of national prosperity. Smith and his contemporaries were therefore happy to make use of evidence from ancient history in developing their theories, to criticise modern states for failing to follow ancient examples in such matters as the treatment of colonies and the organisation of public education, and to think about antiquity in the terms that they had developed to understand their own society. By the middle of the nineteenth century, however, writers with very different views on economic matters were equally convinced that there were fundamental differences between the structure of the modern economy and those of earlier societies. This could be seen clearly in the sheer physical capability of the modern world:

> The bourgeoisie, during its reign of scarce one hundred years, has created more massive and more colossal productive forces than have all preceding generations together. Subjection of Nature's forces to man, machinery, application of chemistry to industry and agriculture, steam-navigation, railways, electric telegraphs, clearing of whole continents for cultivation, canalisation of rivers, whole populations conjured out of the ground – what earlier century had even a presentiment that such productive forces slumbered in the lap of social labour?[4]

> We doubt whether all the exertions of all the inhabitants of the Roman Empire, if exclusively devoted to the manufacture of cotton goods, could, in a whole generation, have produced as great a quantity as is produced each year by a portion of the inhabitants of Lancashire; and we are sure that the produce would have been greatly inferior in quality. The only moving powers employed by the Greeks or Romans were the lower animals, water and wind, and even these powers they used very sparingly.[5]

The consensus was that the vast difference in productive power was due to modern technology and the rational organisation of production. Few writers considered the possibility that there might be differences in the thought processes of ancients and moderns; rather, they continued to assume that 'men we find acting uniformly in all ages, in all counties and in all climates, from the principles of self-interest, expediency, duty or passion', and hence that 'the principles of political economy are eternal and immutable; but one nation is acquainted with them, and another not'.[6]

Most economists in Britain and France thereafter ceased to employ historical evidence and focused on analysis of the modern economy; at the same time they tended to narrow the scope of their research to purely economic matters, whereas the 'political economy' of Adam Smith had encompassed broader issues of political and social organisation. Other writers, however, retained an interest in the historical dimension, and sought to understand the nature of the difference between ancient and modern. Karl Marx focused on the organisation of production and the way in which labour was exploited. He insisted on the fundamental distinction between a society based on slave labour and one in which free workers sold their labour power to capitalists (but were cheated of part of its value): 'The Roman slave was held by chains: the wage-labourer is bound to his owner by invisible threads.'[7] He also insisted that a society based on slave labour could not properly be described as 'capitalist'; that label was reserved for the modern economy. 'In encyclopedias of classical antiquity one can read such nonsense as this: In the ancient world capital was fully developed "except for the absence of the free worker and of a system of credit".'[8] Marx and his followers developed a 'historical materialist' view of history as a series of stages, known as 'modes of production': primitive tribal communism, slavery, feudalism, capitalism.

In late nineteenth-century Germany, a number of other writers went beyond a simple contrast between 'industrial' and 'pre-industrial' societies to develop accounts of the different stages in the economic 'evolution' of humanity. The critical work in this tradition for the development of ancient economic history was Karl Bücher's *Die Entstehung der Volkswirtschaft* [*The Development of the National Economy*], first published in 1893. Bücher's account focused on the location of economic activity, the level of its organisation: European historical development was presented in terms of the three stages of 'household economy', 'city economy' and 'national economy', roughly corresponding to antiquity, the Middle Ages and the modern world.

'Modernising'

Ancient historians had hitherto paid only limited attention to economic matters. The great Theodor Mommsen had offered a highly polemical characterisation of the fall of the Roman Republic as being due to the evils of unbridled capitalism – as he himself put it, 'I wanted to bring down the ancients from the fantastic pedestal on which they appear into the real world' – but this was not based on a careful reading of economic theory.[9] Marx's approach was almost entirely ignored; Bücher's work, however, provoked a furious response from Eduard Meyer, the leading historian of ancient Greece of the time, who objected to what he felt was its demeaning portrayal of antiquity as primitive, the lowest stage of economic development. Bücher had clearly failed to take account of copious evidence for ancient trade and industrial production; it could not reasonably be maintained that the closed household unit was the only form of economic organisation in antiquity. Meyer therefore offered an alternative historical account to emphasise antiquity's achievements, in which the modern development of capitalism out of feudalism had already been prefigured in the history of Greece.

> If the serfdom of the aristocratic epoch of antiquity, of the Homeric period, corresponds to the economic relations of the Christian middle ages, just so the slavery of the following epoch stands on the same level as the free labour of the modern age.[10]

This proved to be the opening salvo in what has become known as the 'modernising' approach to the ancient economy.

This may be summed up by Meyer's remark that 'the later period of antiquity was in essence entirely modern.'[11] The differences between antiquity and the modern world are seen as quantitative rather than qualitative; there was less trade and a lower volume of industrial production in antiquity, but trade and industry were of the same nature, as were the forms of economic organisation and the underlying structures and processes.

> The creation of a uniform world-wide civilization and of similar social and economic conditions is now going on before our eyes over the whole expanse of the civilized world. This process is complicated, and it is often difficult to clear up our minds about it. We ought therefore to keep in view that this condition

in which we are living is not new, and that the ancient world also lived, for a series of centuries, a life which was uniform in culture and politics, in social and economic conditions. The modern development, in this sense, differs from the ancient only in quantity and not in quality.[12]

One might argue that it differs a great deal: modern 'globalisation' (as it is now known) is driven mainly by developments in communication technology and the demands of multinational corporations, rather than by the conquests of an imperial power. As ever, it is a question of whether the differences between two historical societies seem more striking than the similarities; 'modernisers' tend to be most aware of possible parallels.

In the cities we find an industrial system which in many respects resembles that of early nineteenth-century New England where the native artisans of inland towns not yet connected by steam power produced most of the articles needed by each town. However, many of the Roman cities were now growing large and the number of wealthy men who demanded and could pay for luxuries and delicacies far exceeded that of our early Republic. To gratify these an extensive commerce had long existed, and in some lines of production industries aiming at a world market had already arisen.[13]

In evaluating such accounts, we need to take account not just of their substantive assertions (the growth of Roman cities, the development of industry) but also of the concepts being employed (for example, the phrase 'industrial system' has very different connotations from 'craft production') and the underlying assumptions (for example, that there was a 'world market' which influenced economic decisions).

'Modernising' is not a coherent theoretical position so much as a kind of historical temperament, a disposition to interpret the ancient evidence optimistically. Modernisers tend to be struck by how much evidence there is rather than by how little. They have little time for arguments from silence, preferring to offer theories to explain why particular evidence has not survived: for example, the lack of evidence for Roman senators whose family fortunes were based on trade might be explained by the fact, suggested by comparative evidence from early modern France, that such nouveaux riches might do their best to suppress any trace of their disreputable origins.[14] The evidence that has survived is always assumed to point to a much larger amount of activity in antiquity and is almost invariably attributed to market-oriented, entrepreneurial activity rather than to low-level self-sufficiency. For example, the evidence for cloth production in Pompeii is assumed to relate to an export-oriented wool industry rather than to small-scale workshops catering for local consumers; Greek colonies must have been founded for the sake of trade, cities must have pursued deliberate policies of encouraging exports and promoting local industry, ancient capitalists must have become wealthy and influential in their cities.[15] No explicit argument is offered to justify using modern terminology such as 'capitalism', 'entrepreneur', 'market' or 'industrial system'; they are simply deployed as being the natural terms with which to discuss the subject. The achievement of antiquity is emphasised: 'Never before had so considerable a part of Europe, Asia and Africa presented an aspect so civilized, so modern, one may say, in its essential features.'[16]

'Primitivism'

'Modernisers' rarely claim that label for themselves; it is generally attributed to a particular work by its critics, on the basis of its allegedly 'modernising' assumptions and concepts. Such critics would in turn only rarely identify themselves as 'primitivists', the label often applied to them. Rather, historians of either persuasion would claim simply to be offering an accurate picture of the ancient world, in contrast to the excessive optimism – or excessive pessimism – of others.

The majority of historians associated with 'primitivism' argued not so much that antiquity was 'primitive' as that it was very definitely 'not modern'. This approach can trace its roots back to the work of Marx, Bücher and other nineteenth-century historical economists, but it is first clearly articulated in the responses of Max Weber and Johannes Hasebroek to the modernising account of Meyer. Weber, much of whose work focused on trying to explain the rise of capitalism in early modern Europe, emphasised the contrast between antiquity and the Middle Ages. He sought to explain the former's failure to develop into a full-blown capitalist economy by focusing on the ways in which ancient economic activity was organised (including, as we have seen, the particular nature of the ancient 'consumer' city compared with the medieval 'producer'). Hasebroek followed this line of argument and insisted on the importance of understanding Greek trade in the context of city politics, especially the fact that trade was left to non-citizens who were excluded from political activity; ancient states never attempted to promote trade but focused simply on ensuring adequate food supplies. The casual assumption that ancient economic activity was comparable with modern is comprehensively rejected; the differences between the two societies are seen to be qualitative, a matter of the nature and structural location of trade and manufacturing, not merely quantitative. Antiquity was not modern; it was an interesting case study for Weber precisely because, for all its sophistication, it had entirely failed to provide a platform for economic development.

The ideas of Weber and Hasebroek were largely ignored by ancient historians, with the field dominated instead until after the Second World War by the 'modernising' histories of writers such as M.I. Rostovtzeff and Tenney Frank. In the second half of the twentieth century, however, Weber's ideas were revived and the 'primitivist' approach became widespread and highly influential, if never wholly dominant. A.H.M. Jones developed a much more careful, and pessimistic, account of the limitations of the evidence for the ancient economy and hence the limits on what historians were able sensibly to discuss. M.I. Finley offered similar scepticism about the sources, especially archaeological data (which had fuelled much of Rostovtzeff's enthusiastic estimation of the Roman economy), and gave the lectures that were published as *The Ancient Economy* in 1973: still the definitive anti-modernising account of antiquity, and the inspiration for a range of important studies in the 1970s and 1980s.

Finley's account of antiquity in *The Ancient Economy* can sometimes seem rather negative, as one key part of his message is to emphasise constantly the absence of features associated with a modern economy: economic rationality, integrated price-making markets, free wage labour, technological innovation, large-scale industrial enterprises, state intervention in the economy, and so forth. In this respect it was a book of its time, intended to combat the then widespread misconceptions of the more extreme modernisers; its success in forcing all historians, of whatever persuasion, to be more careful about their assumptions now makes that aspect of the argument appear rather overstated. In fact, Finley also offers a powerful characterisation of the ancient economy as 'embedded' in ancient society and culture. Of the ancients' failure to develop the discipline of economics, he remarks: 'it becomes essential to ask whether this is merely accidental, an intellectual failing, a problem in the history of ideas in the narrow sense, or whether it is a consequence of the structure of ancient society'. His answer is the latter: it is not just that the ancients saw the world differently, with a blind spot where we identify economic processes; their world actually worked differently. Ancient economic activity can only be understood in the context of ancient society, unlike the modern world, in which it operates as a separate sector of society.

Thus, rather than being organised around such topics as agriculture, industry and trade, *The Ancient Economy* offers chapters on 'Orders and status', 'Masters and slaves' and 'Town and country'. The ancients, Finley argues, made economic decisions not on the modern basis of profit and loss or comparative advantage but according to social and cultural norms concerning political status and the ideal of self-sufficiency. This is certainly what we find in the vast majority of the sources; the few ancient attempts at rational calculation – the classic example is the attempt of the Roman agricultural writer Columella to demonstrate the profitability of vine growing – are, by modern standards, laughably inept. The landowning elite – who were the only group in a position to invest in economic development – regarded manual labour as demeaning, even slavish, and trade as risky and rather vulgar; agriculture alone was socially acceptable, and even there they aimed at satisfying needs rather than maximising returns. The dominance of these aristocratic values throughout the ancient world (which, incidentally, justifies the decision to treat 'the ancient economy' as a unity rather than separating the Roman from the Greek or Carthaginian) explains its failure to develop. Technology, for example, is held back by a range of factors, all of which can be traced back to the elite worldview: the abstract theoretical approach of ancient science, the view of man as part of nature rather than nature existing to be exploited by man, the lack of funding for productive technology (as opposed to gadgets, such as the use of steam power to open temple doors automatically), since there was no incentive to save labour in a society that employed slaves because they enhanced their owner's status. In every respect this is contrasted implicitly (as Weber had contrasted it explicitly) with the medieval situation, which had laid the foundations for economic transformation.

Other writers in this tradition have produced complementary characterisations of the limitations of the ancient economy by looking to material factors: above all, its reliance on human and animal power rather than steam, placing limitations on the level of surplus production and hence on the level of demand for goods. Antiquity is characterised not as 'primitive' but as 'underdeveloped', by analogy with countries in the modern 'developing world'.

> The Roman economy was underdeveloped. This means essentially that the mass of the population lived at or near subsistence level. In a typical underdeveloped, pre-industrial economy, a large proportion of the labour force is employed in agriculture, which is the main avenue for investment and source of wealth. The level of investment in manufacturing industry is low. Resources that might in theory be devoted to growth-inducing investment are directed into consumption or into unproductive speculation and usury. Demand for manufactured goods is relatively low, and most needs are met locally with goods made by small craftsmen at home. Backward technology is a further barrier to increased productivity. Finally, there is no class of entrepreneurs who are both capable of perceiving opportunities for profit in large-scale organisation of manufacture and prepared to undergo the risks entailed in making the necessary investment.[17]

> The scale of inter-regional trade was very small. Overland transport was too expensive, except for the cartage of luxury goods. And even by sea, trade constituted only a very small proportion of gross product. This was partly because each region in the Mediterranean basin had a roughly similar climate and so grew similar crops. The low level of long-distance trade was also due to the fact that neither economies of scale nor investment in productive techniques ever reduced unit production costs sufficiently to compensate for high transport costs. Therefore no region or town could specialize in the manufacture of cheaper goods; it could only export prestige goods, even overseas. And finally the market for such prestige goods was necessarily limited by the poverty of most city-dwellers and peasants.[18]

The key theme here is that of the limits on ancient economic performance: low demand, low productivity, low investment, not much trade. It would be conceded that, compared with other pre-industrial societies, Greece and Rome were in some respects quite advanced and sophisticated; but, to counteract the tendency to view the past through our own experiences, the stress remains on the vast gulf between ancient and modern.

Formalism and substantivism

Modernisers and primitivists offer different accounts of what the ancient world was like, based on competing interpretations of the sources. Running alongside this debate, and intersecting with it regularly, is a theoretical dispute about how the ancient economy (and other non-modern economies) should be studied, and what sorts of categories and concepts should be employed in interpreting the evidence. The opposing positions are often known as 'formalism' and 'substantivism', the labels devised when these issues became the focus of argument in the field of economic anthropology (the study of economic activities in contemporary non-Western countries) in the decades after the Second World War.

The basic issue at stake was whether modern neoclassical economic theory should be employed in the study of non-Western, pre-modern economies. Formalists argued that economic theory is universally applicable: all societies have to contend with scarcity and hence need to make decisions about the best allocation of resources (labour time, land, capital resources); human beings are rational, and will therefore make these decisions on the rational basis of max-imising utility. Substantivists argued on the contrary that economic theory was developed to study the modern capitalist economy and so is useless for non-capitalist and non-Western economies in which the economy is 'embedded' in social structures. It was noted that the economy is not wholly separable from society even today, but it was in the study of pre-modern societies that the assumptions of economic theory about human behaviour seemed most unrealistic. Faced with a society that did not value land in purely financial terms (for example, restricting ownership to certain privileged groups such as higher castes or citizens), or did not cost labour inputs, or preferred to satisfy needs and minimise risk rather than maximise profits, modern economics could only dismiss such behaviour as 'ir-rational' in their terms; substantivists aim to produce an analysis that is more culturally sensitive and specific.

'Formalism versus substantivism' amounts to the following theoretical option: between the ready-made models of orthodox Economics, especially the 'microeconomics', taken as universally valid and applicable grosso modo to the primitive societies; and the necessity – supposing this formalist position unfounded – of developing a new analysis more appropriate to the historical societies in question . . . Broadly speaking, it is a choice between the perspective of Business, for the formalist method must consider the primitive economies as underdeveloped versions of our own, and a culturalist study that as a matter of principle does honour to different societies for what they are.[19]

There is clearly a lot of common ground between the substantivists and the primitivists, both insisting on the 'difference' of non-modern economies, and many of the historians associated with primitivism – Finley most notably – pursued a substantivist approach to the study of antiquity. The basic message of *The Ancient Economy* was that modern economic terms are unsuitable, and that any analysis of the ancient economy must be conducted in 'culturalist' terms, paying attention to the ways that the ancients themselves conceived of their world. Historians in this tradition have looked beyond economics for ways of interpreting ancient economic behaviour: to the sociology of Max Weber, in the case of Finley, and to anthropology.

There is equally an overlap between formalism and a modernising approach to antiquity, though proponents of the latter have often employed modern concepts on the basis of a careless assumption that ancient and modern were essentially similar, rather than a coherent formalist argument. As Finley commented:

> The relationship between trade and politics in classical Greece still seems to be treated most of the time as if there were no conceptual problems, as if, in Rostovtzeff's language, it is only a question of facts. And that means, necessarily, that the concepts and generalisations which are constantly being brought to bear, expressly or tacitly, are modern ones, even when they hide beneath the mask of 'common sense'.[20]

Substantivism is plainly incompatible with a modernising view of antiquity. Formalism and primitivism, however, are not so wholly antipathetic; one might plausibly hold both that economic theory does reveal universally valid principles and that in material terms the ancient world was underdeveloped. This is indeed the position of Hopkins in his 'taxes and trade' model and elsewhere. If this approach is accepted, some economic principles are likely to be more useful than others; microeconomics, dealing with decision making at the level of the individual estate or enterprise, may seem more relevant to antiquity than theories of international exchange rates, given that the ancient economy was apparently poorly integrated. The key point is that, according to this approach, economic theories are to be evaluated by their usefulness, the extent to which they can offer a persuasive interpretation of the evidence, rather than being automatically ruled invalid and unacceptable. They offer ideas as to how things might have operated, rather than a statement of how they must have been; to employ them it is not necessary to assume that ancient world was modern but simply that it was sufficiently comparable to the idealised world of the economic model.

The politics of ancient economics

The ancient economy, like most of the rest of ancient history, is not an obvious focus for bitter political arguments. Economic anthropology, however, has always been a politically contentious subject, since its research is used to influence and to justify the policies of national governments, aid agencies and organisations such as the World Bank and the International Monetary Fund towards countries in the Third World. Theories on the nature of 'economic development' determine how money will be spent, and what sorts of projects will receive funding. Policies over the last fifty years have been driven by the assumption that such countries should be pushed to imitate the industrialised West as rapidly as possible: they promote large-scale capital projects such as dams and irrigation, massive industrialisation, market-oriented agricultural production in place of subsistence farming, free movement of capital and the privatisation of state enterprises. One policy is offered for all situations, as clearly the modern European experience provides the blueprint for economic growth and national prosperity.

Substantivism developed in opposition to this approach. It rejects the underlying assumption that there is a single model of economic development and hence tends to reject the term 'developing countries'. Western arrogance, it is argued, has ignored the possibility that traditional practices might have been better suited to local environmental conditions; Western governments blame corruption and ignorance when their reforms fail, whereas in fact they failed because alien practices were simply imposed on a society that operated according to quite different norms. Formalist economic theory is blamed for the poverty, the displacement of millions of people, the environmental damage and the crippling levels of debt that its policies have created in many regions, but there are still more serious accusations: economics' 'colonisation' of the intellectual field, dismissing traditional practices as irrational and backwards, is said to have served to justify the appropriation of resources by Western corporations on the grounds of their superior expertise. In turn, the substantivists are accused of *naïveté*, of wishing to prevent non-Western countries from benefiting from economic progress, and of having communist and/or anarchistic revolutionary sympathies.

In some cases, especially within the Marxist tradition, these political arguments have been extended into the past: the economy of classical antiquity becomes equally politicised. As we have seen, Marx emphasised the power of a particular vocabulary to shape the world in its own image: if antiquity is labelled 'capitalist', it creates the impression that capitalism is an 'eternal law of nature', hence the natural way of doing things. Alternative forms of economic organisation are thus implicitly shown to be unnatural, and hence undesirable. Marx insists on the 'difference' of the past as a means of showing that capitalism has not always existed – and so may not always exist in future. Classical antiquity was a highly sophisticated society; its example demonstrates that we do not face a simple choice between capitalism and barbarism but that new and better forms of society are possible. The past offers hope for the revolution of the future; in the meantime, we should resist attempts by the apologists for big business to colonise the past.

Economic theory, it is clear, is not a neutral science but an ideological position. Of course, the same is clearly true of the substantivist approach. Besides its affiliation to radical politics, it is sometimes prone to idealise the spirituality and authenticity of non-Western societies, and to suffer from nostalgia for an (imaginary) pre-industrial rural paradise (as seen for example in William Morris, another intellectual forerunner). It does not always escape the Western tendency to regard anything different as inherently inferior, and so it does not always succeed in preventing 'not modern' from becoming 'primitive'.

> This essential distance from the past can come to resemble a clumsy lurch to save oneself from overbalancing on one side, which ends up in a fall on the other. Distancing ourselves is thus a necessary but not a sufficient condition for a balanced

judgement. Stopping obstinately here, one can certainly avoid 'modernism', but cannot avoid falling head long into the more common but hardly less harmful defect of 'primitivism'. Instead of claiming that the dead are like us (Columella is a capitalist) we end up claiming that they are inferior to us (Columella can't keep his books). 'Modernism' and 'primitivism' are two sides to the same coin, the self-deification of the present and the annihilation of the past.[21]

Weber and Finley both tend to see antiquity in terms of its failure to develop into a modern capitalist economy, in contrast to the later Middle Ages. It is certainly valid to explore, as Weber did, the reasons why the ancient economy did not develop in this way, but it is not the only interesting question to ask. It is also potentially misleading if it assumes, as Weber and Finley tended to, that this was the only path antiquity could have taken, that the only alternatives were development on the model of early modern Europe or economic stagnation.

A further problem with most histories of technology is that only those items that led to modern western 'high' technology are considered really interesting. Anything military or mechanical is always valued above the ingenuity of ordinary ceramics, textiles or basketwork, despite the greater benefit of the latter to a larger number of people. Likewise, almost everything is judged in terms of saving time and labour, which are unlikely to have been conceptualised, let alone commoditised, in anything like the same manner in pre-industrial societies.[22]

Viewing antiquity only in terms of the modern/not-modern dichotomy may be equally misleading and limited regardless of whether it is then judged a success or a failure.

Histories of economic development offer a particular set of stories about humanity and about our relation to the past. The vast majority have been highly optimistic and teleological, figuring the modern world as the culmination of a long process of technical ingenuity, hard work and entrepreneurial initiative, to create the conditions for wealth and prosperity. Antiquity plays the role of a missed opportunity or a false dawn (the modernisers), or just part of the long prologue before true economic growth became possible. There is room for alternative stories: for Marshall Sahlins's substantivist account of 'the original affluent society', suggesting that 'primitive' hunter–gatherers were actually better off than farmers, let alone industrial workers, or for accounts of the ancient world that discern the possibility of an entirely different history.

New approaches

Recently, ancient economic history has enjoyed something of a revival, after a period in which all the most exciting research seemed to be taking place in other fields while the economic debate remained stuck in the rut of the primitivists versus modernisers, Finley right or wrong debate. So far this revival has been manifested in journal articles and collections of papers from conferences rather than would-be definitive books, and it is characterised by the wide range of different approaches rather than by a single dominant interpretation or a clear division between opposing camps. The majority of participants seem to share a certain amount of common ground, much of it the legacy of Finley's work; they accept the characterisation of classical antiquity as 'pre-industrial', vastly inferior in productive power to the modern world and organised on quite different lines, while also noting its relative sophistication compared with most other pre-industrial societies. There seems to be widespread agreement that the most interesting topic to explore is not the ancient economy's failure to develop but its particular structure and organisation, its own laws of motion – not to be studied in isolation, since the limitations of the ancient evidence mean that there will always be a need for comparative material to help develop interpretations, but not wholly focused on the modern/not-modern dichotomy.

Some fundamental issues remain unresolved: above all, what is an appropriate choice of vocabulary for describing ancient economic activity, given that no vocabulary can be wholly neutral? Some historians maintain the formalist position that economic principles, especially if employed with a clear sense of their logical status as models, not laws, provide a better understanding of how the economy actually worked than the limited concepts of the historical participants. Some recent developments in economic theory have also made it more amenable to use by historians. Having traditionally treated the economy as something entirely separate from and unaffected by society, economists now pay more attention to the role of social institutions – the state, the legal system, even religion – in encouraging exchange by reducing the costs of enforcing agreements between buyer and seller. Others have developed studies of the role of subjective preferences, political and social and cultural factors – in conventional economic terms, 'irrationality' – in decision making, with the aim of refining economic models rather than basing them on untenable assumptions about human motivation. Some areas of economics, at least, are becoming more 'culturalist' in their approach even to the modern economy; by reducing the strength of their claims to absolute knowledge, they may prove more useful and certainly more acceptable (or at least less unacceptable) to sceptical ancient historians.

Some of these historians, however, continue to resist the implicit modernising involved in any use of economic terminology and insist on the primacy of what are sometimes termed the actors' categories: the ways that the Greeks and Romans themselves conceived the world naturally shaped their actions. 'Trade', for example, is not an abstract concept but a particular sort of activity founded on certain kinds of social relationship. Indeed, anthropological material has long revealed the complexity and multifariousness of such activities, going far beyond the purely 'economic':

> In the systems of the past we do not find simple exchange of goods, wealth and produce through markets established among individuals. For it is groups, and not individuals, which carry on exchange, make contracts, and are bound by obligations . . . Further, what they exchange is not exclusively goods and wealth, real and personal property, and things of economic value. They exchange rather courtesies, entertainments, ritual, military assistance, women, children, dances and feasts; and fairs in which the market is but one element and the circulation of wealth but one part of a wide and enduring contract.[23]

To study trade (or agriculture, or manufacturing, or money) in purely economic terms may be intellectually convenient, but it completely misses all the other dimensions, all the other meanings of the activity, most of which were far more important to the ancients than the purely economic.

> While in conventional economic analysis the market stands for a certain kind of exchange which functions independently of the culture by which it is surrounded, the ancient *agora* was firmly embedded in the value-system of the *polis*.[24]

Conventional economic analysis is limited, partially sighted, and hence highly misleading.

These debates will continue. New evidence for the ancient economy continues to emerge, above all through the labours of papyrologists and archaeologists, but it cannot resolve the disputes about the best way to study the subject, the proper framework of interpretation. Archaeology can show, for example, that so many amphorae of wine were moved from Italy to Gaul in the first century BCE; it is less successful in showing who moved them, whether this was trade or some form of redistribution, and what this meant, in economic or cultural terms – let alone whether the economic or the cultural meaning is more important. That depends on a whole range of assumptions, not just about the relation between ancient and modern but about the place of 'the economy' in the modern world. Do we regard Aristotle's ignorance of economics with a certain amount of contempt, because of his intellectual failure or the limitations of his society, or with a certain amount of longing, because the Greeks were able to keep economic matters in their proper place rather than enthroning them as the ultimate determinant of human life? This is not a question that ancient economic historians tend to ask themselves explicitly, but such issues undoubtedly influence their interpretations.

Chapter 3

The limits of the possible

Materialism

The dispute between formalists and substantivists is by no means the only theoretical issue underlying discussions of the ancient economy, although it has tended to claim the most attention from historians. Another key difference is the question of whether human development should be conceived primarily in 'idealist' or 'materialist' terms – or rather, as it is clearly a mixture of both, which one should be given explanatory precedence. What kinds of factors determine the course of human history?

The idealist approach is most often associated with the German philosopher G.W.F. Hegel, who, in lectures delivered at the beginning of the nineteenth century, presented human history as a story of the development of reason and self-consciousness.[1] For example, an institution such as ancient slavery is presented as the material expression of the Greek worldview (Zeitgeist, the state of consciousness of a particular historical stage), that some (but not all) men are free. This is (for Hegel) an advance on the previous stage of consciousness, which assumed that only one man (the king or tyrant) was free, but was in due course to be superseded by the Christian view that all men are free under God, which was now being replaced in turn with the modern view that all men are free absolutely.

Even more than most grand theories of historical development, Hegel's account is highly abstract and schematic, paying little attention to the details of the evidence. However, it does exemplify the view that ideas, thoughts and beliefs are the driving force of historical change, shaping the material world by shaping human perceptions and actions. Echoes of this approach can be found in Max Weber's account of the rise of capitalism in late medieval and early modern Europe, which places great stress on the role of the value system of

Protestant Christianity – the belief in predestination, the emphasis on the virtues of hard work and thrift – in creating the conditions for economic development.[2]

> Not ideas, but material and ideal interests, directly govern men's conduct. Yet very frequently the 'world images' that have been created by 'ideas' have, like switchmen, determined the tracks along which action has been pushed by the dynamic of interest.[3]

Similarly, Finley's stress on the role of ideas and ideals, such as status and self-sufficiency, in shaping the economic activities of antiquity, and on the implications of the absence from antiquity of 'economic rationality', exemplifies a modified 'idealist' approach. Material factors are not discounted, but they are treated, implicitly or explicitly, as secondary.

The opposing position, materialism, emphasises the way that the material world shapes people's perceptions of it. Karl Marx and his collaborator Frederick Engels, the doyens of this approach, provide its clearest (or certainly most quotable) justification:

> In direct contrast to German philosophy which descends from heaven to earth, here it is a matter of ascending from earth to heaven. That is to say, not of setting out from what men say, imagine, conceive, not from men as narrated, thought of, imagine, conceived, in order to arrive at men in the flesh; but setting out from real, active men, and on the basis of their real life-process demonstrating the development of the ideological reflexes and echoes of this life-process. The phantoms formed in the brains of men are also, necessarily, sublimates of their material life-process, which is empirically verifiable and bound to material premises.[4]

Marx and Engels set themselves in direct opposition to the Hegelian approach, and so, in this passage at least, tend to overstate their case. They do not always discount ideas as 'phantoms' – but they do insist on the primacy of the material.

> We must begin by stating the first premise of all human existence and, therefore, of all history, the premise, namely, that men must be in a position to live in order to be able to 'make

history'. But life involves before everything else eating and drinking, housing, clothing and various other things. The first historical act is thus the production of the means to satisfy these needs, the production of material life itself.[5]

Debate continues, both within Marxism and between Marxists and their critics, on the question of how far the material 'base' of society determines the 'superstructure' of ideas, culture, social relations, and so forth. A common criticism of historical materialism is that it is 'determinist'; that is to say, it denies any role for chance, or free will, or the individual and his/her perceptions, in shaping the course of events. Weber's comments on the role of ideas in shaping behaviour, quoted above, are in part a response to Marx, who might in turn happily concede the point but insist on focusing on the material conditions that had shaped those ideas. 'The Middle Ages could not live on Catholicism, nor could the ancient world on politics.'[6]

For most historians, the balance between material and ideal factors in historical explanation remains a matter of (often unconscious) subjective preference: what sorts of explanation seem to explain best? The issues are more prominent in some areas of history than others; arguably, a preference for cultural rather than economic history may simply reflect an inclination for idealist rather than materialist approaches. The debate is difficult to avoid in the topic discussed in this chapter, the use of modern research in the social and biological sciences to explore how human history has been shaped by processes beyond the consciousness of individuals – the impersonal forces of nature, and the workings of their own bodies.

La longue durée

There is in fact a long tradition of studying the effects of climate and terrain on history. Herodotus followed other Greek writers in arguing that cold makes men savage and ungovernable whereas heat makes them indolent and slavish; Greece, situated midway between Europe and Asia, naturally produces the best men. This approach survived well into the twentieth century, with the idea that only temperate (European) climates are capable of producing 'civilisation'. Mainstream history was as ever wary of such grand (and, from a modern perspective, politically dubious) theories; it remained focused on the history of events, of politics and wars, in which the natural world, if it was noticed at all, served simply as background, the terrain across which people made history.

The first sign of a proper engagement between history and geography came in France in the 1920s, when Marc Bloch and Lucien Febvre founded the journal *Annales d'histoire économique et sociale* (known today as *Annales ESC*, standing for *Economies, Sociétés, Civilisations*).[7] The journal was intended to encourage and promote 'their sort of history': focusing on economic and social history rather than politics, drawing on contemporary work in the social sciences and making extensive use of comparative evidence. Their work, and that of others in what became known as the 'Annales School', concentrated on the analysis of 'structures' rather than the narrative of events, aiming to produce 'total history', encompassing the whole range of human activities. Bloch pioneered the study of *mentalité* (see Chapter 6), while Febvre wrote *A Geographical Introduction to History* (1925), intended to emphasise the importance of climate and terrain in shaping historical events, while avoiding the excessive determinism of previous versions of 'geographical history'.

> Either the living being is more or less passive under the action of the natural forces of its environment, and we can calculate its reaction with certainty and therefore foresee it by measuring its powers of resistance to the measurable forces opposing it. Or else the living being is endowed with an activity of its own and capable of creating and producing new effects, in which case there is an end of determination in the true sense of the word; and in its place we have only approximations and probabilities. We lose, on the one hand, much of the beautiful simplicity and certainty of the mechanical explanations. We gain on the other hand . . . a richer and more complex view, better matched with the exact complexion of the phenomena of life.[8]

However, the name most commonly associated with a geographical approach to history is that of Fernand Braudel, who became Febvre's successor as head of the Ecole des Hautes Etudes en Sciences Sociales in Paris (Bloch had been killed during the Second World War). This is above all on account of his book *The Mediterranean and the Mediterranean World in the Age of Philip II*, first published in 1949, one of the classic historical works of the twentieth century. Rather than being a history focused on the activities of individuals, in Braudel's account the Mediterranean Sea itself becomes the key protagonist, shaping the lives of Philip II and every other inhabitant of the region.

This book is divided into three parts, each of which is itself an essay in general explanation.

The first part is devoted to a history in which all change is slow, a history of constant repetition, ever-recurring cycles. I could not neglect this almost timeless history, the story of man's contact with the inanimate, neither could I be satisfied with the traditional geographical introduction to history that often figures to little purpose at the beginning of so many books, with its descriptions of the mineral deposits, types of agriculture, and typical flora, briefly listed and never mentioned again, as if the flowers did not come back every spring, the flocks of sheep migrate every year, or the ships sail on a real sea that changes with the seasons.

On a different level from the first there can be distinguished another history, this time with slow but perceptible rhythms. If the expression had not been diverted from its full meaning, one could call it *social history*, the history of groups and groupings. How did these swelling currents affect Mediterranean life in general . . . ?

Lastly, the third part gives a hearing to traditional history – history, one might say, on the scale not of man, but of individual men . . . *l'histoire événementielle*, that is, the history of events: surface disturbances, crests of foam that the tides of history carry on their strong backs. A history of brief, rapid, nervous fluctuations, by definition ultra-sensitive; the least tremor sets all its antennae quivering. But as such it is the most exciting of all, the richest in human interest, and also the most dangerous.[9]

As Braudel notes, history has traditionally focused on events: dramatic, short-term and – by implication – trivial, mere surface froth. Economic and social history, along with economics and sociology, studies the deeper forces that shape events in the medium term. It is pointless to study such processes at the level of a day or a week: changes take place over years and decades. Braudel, however, insists on the importance of still deeper currents, influencing the structures of human society over centuries and even millennia.

The final effect then is to dissect history into various planes, or, to put it another way, to divide historical time into geographical time, social time, and individual time. Or, alternatively, to divide man into a multitude of selves.[10]

This tripartite division – rather than, say, distinguishing also between changes over decades and changes over centuries – is clearly arbitrary; as Braudel notes, 'these levels I have distinguished are only means of exposition'.[11] Clearly these different levels of change, these different sorts of historical time, influence one another in both directions: *l'histoire événementielle* can affect the course of medium-term economic and social processes, and (as the early twenty-first century has become all too aware) cumulative human activity can affect even the structures of *la longue durée*, the climate and the environment. The historian's task is to explore and analyse these complex interactions, 'to define a hierarchy of forces, of currents, of particular movements, and then tackle them as an entire constellation.'[12] It is clear that for Braudel the hierarchy of explanatory importance must privilege the vast, impersonal, almost irresistible forces of nature over the more 'human' time of individuals and social processes. That demands a complete change of focus on the part of the historian, a new view of historical causation and a new way of thinking and writing about the past.

> Among the different sorts of historical time, the *longue durée* often seems a troublesome character, full of complications, and all too frequently lacking in any sort of organization. To give it a place in the heart of our profession would entail more than a routine expansion of our studies and our curiosities. Nor would it be a question of making a simple choice in its favor. For the historian, accepting the *longue durée* entails a readiness to change his style, his attitudes, a whole reversal in his thinking, a whole new way of conceiving of social affairs.[13]

Braudel's *Mediterranean* offers a powerful vision of the influence of the environment on history, a radically different perspective on the past. It is an unforgettable book, which according to one commentator 'has a good claim to be regarded as the most important work of history of the century', but its theoretical framework has also received some fierce criticism.[14] It is striking how far the equally monumental and all-encompassing book on the Mediterranean by Horden and Purcell, *The Corrupting Sea*, is concerned to distance itself from Braudel's approach.

Angelus

The Angel of the Lord declared to Mary:
And she conceived of the Holy Spirit. Hail Mary...

Behold the handmaid of the Lord: Be it done
Unto me according to Thy word. Hail Mary...

And the Word was made Flesh: And dwelt
among us. Hail Mary...

Pray for us, O Holy Mother of God, that we may
be made worthy of the promises of Christ.

Let us pray: Pour forth, we beseech Thee, O
Lord, Thy grace into our hearts; that
we, to whom the incarnation of
Christ, Thy Son, was made known by
the message of an angel, may by His
passion and Cross be brought to the
glory of His Resurrection, through the
same Christ Our Lord.

Amen

The first and most obvious criticism is that Braudel downplays the role of the individual in history; his vision verges on geographical determinism:

> When I think of the individual, I am always inclined to see him imprisoned within a destiny in which he himself has little hand, fixed in a landscape in which the infinite perspectives of the long term stretch into the distance both behind him and before. In historical analysis, as I see it, rightly or wrongly, the long run always wins in the end. Annihilating innumerable events – all those which cannot be accommodated in the main ongoing current and which are therefore ruthlessly swept to one side – it indubitably limits both the freedom of the individual and even the role of chance.[15]

It has been suggested that this vision must owe something to the circumstances of its composition, while Braudel was imprisoned in a German prisoner-of-war camp. This might be seen in optimistic terms – the long run always wins in the end, the Nazis cannot conquer geography – or as an expression of frustrated inactivity (compare the individual-centred existentialist philosophy of Braudel's contemporary Jean-Paul Sartre, who spent the war assisting the Resistance). Braudel does not in fact argue for an absolute determinism but, following Febvre, a sense of the limits that *la longue durée* places on the individual's freedom of action, employing the Annales School's favourite metaphor of 'structure':

> By *structure*, observers of social questions mean an organization, a coherent and fairly fixed series of relationships between realities and social masses. For us historians, a structure is of course a construct, an architecture, but over and above that it is a reality which time uses and abuses over long periods. Some structures, because of their long life, become stable elements for an infinite number of generations: they get in the way of history, hinder its flow, and in hindering shape it. Others wear themselves out more quickly. But all of them provide both support and hindrance. As hindrances they stand as limits . . . beyond which man and his experiences cannot go. Just think of the difficulties of breaking out of certain geographical frameworks, certain biological realities, certain limits of productivity, even

particular spiritual constraints: mental frameworks too can form prisons of the *longue durée*.

> Can it not be said that there is a limit, a ceiling which restricts all human life, containing it within a frontier of varying outline, one which is hard to reach and harder still to cross? This is the border which in every age, even our own, separates the possible from the impossible, what can be done with a little effort from what cannot be done at all.[16]

Part of the historian's task, then, is to identify and analyse the structures that organise and limit human activity. For the ancient world, we might explore such topics as the influence of geography on travel and communication, and its consequences: the restricted sailing season, the high cost and slow speed of land travel, the concentration of major cities at the coasts or on navigable rivers, the importance of mountains and deserts as impediments to communication – the exceptional case, such as Hannibal crossing the Alps with his elephants, simply highlighting how far these barriers normally hinder human activity and how great an effort is required to breach them.

Braudel's ideas have proved particularly influential in the field of survey archaeology, studying changing patterns of settlement and land use within a region over long periods of time.[17] They emphasise the classical world's dependence on agriculture, and thus on the weather, in an environment characterised by enormous variations in rainfall and temperature; we can now see how antiquity oscillated unpredictably between glut and dearth, always hovering on the edge of disaster and having to develop strategies (agricultural techniques such as mixed farming, social relationships such as friendship and patronage, economic and political measures such as grain imports) to minimise risk.[18] Nature was not all-powerful – indeed, some of the most interesting topics to explore are precisely the ways in which the Greeks and Romans sought to overcome its limits – but it established the day-to-day rhythms of existence, the material reality that determined (for example) how often Athenian farmers could attend the Assembly or how easily Greek states could mount overseas campaigns.

The second major complaint about Braudel's approach to history is that the picture tends to be very static; his emphasis on the almost unchanging structures of *la longue durée*, although an important corrective to traditional event-centred accounts, does beg the question of why it is that change does in fact occur. Given Braudel's insistence, at least in his theoretical discussions, on the importance of exploring the connections between the different levels of historical time, there is no reason to think that this immobility is intrinsic to his approach. Rather, he is simply not especially interested in such questions. For example, in one of his later books he presents a comparative history of the great food plants of the world.

> Wherever it began, agriculture had from the start been obliged to opt for one of the major food-plants; and had been built up around this initial choice of priority on which everything or almost everything would thereafter depend. Three of these plants were brilliantly successful: wheat, rice and maize. They continue to share world arable land between them today. The 'plants of civilization', they have profoundly organized man's material and sometimes his spiritual life, to the point where they have become almost ineradicable structures.[19]

This is classic Braudel in the way that it brings into the foreground the everyday, the taken-for-granted, the aspects of life that actually dominated the lives of the vast majority of people in the past. Implicit in the midst of copious information about agricultural techniques, culinary practices, and so forth is the suggestion that the main food crops of different regions influenced the destinies of the civilisations that arose there.

> Without maize, the giant Mayan or Aztec pyramids, the cyclopean walls of Cuzco or the wonders of Machu Pichu would have been impossible. They were achieved because maize virtually produces itself. The problem then is that on one hand we have a series of striking achievements, on the other, human misery. As usual we must ask: who is to blame. Man of course. But maize as well.[20]

Braudel does not develop the implications of these ideas – for example, that the triumph of Europe might be attributed to its reliance on wheat rather than rice or maize – any further than these vague hints. As Horden and Purcell commented of *The Mediterranean*, his work is 'more panoramic than problem-solving', offering quantities of fascinating information and evocative anecdotes but little explicit analysis.[21]

This is frustrating; but it may also be taken as a challenge, to follow through Braudel's project and to explore how the structures of *la longue durée* have shaped human society through time. We know that the environment can change over the course of a century or two; the Braudelian perspective compels us to consider the consequences. Sometimes these changes are the result of human activity; this is more often associated with the modern world and its awesome technological capability, but one historian has attributed the decline of the ancient world to the Romans' destruction of the natural environment:

> Nonrenewable resources were consumed, and renewable resources were exploited faster than was sustainable. As a result, the lands where Western civilization received its formative impulse were gradually drained, losing their living and nonliving heritage. This was the fate of the natural environment and human populations alike, and it was not something that came irresistibly from outside with a climatic change or other natural disaster; it was the result of the unwise actions of the Greeks and Romans themselves, unwitting as they may have been.[22]

Other historians have criticised this view, suggesting that the evidence for ancient deforestation and environmental degradation has been grossly exaggerated.[23] But that does not exclude the possibility that the environment played a key role in the collapse of the western Roman Empire, whether because climatic changes in the depths of Asia triggered mass movements of tribes – one theory as to why settled agricultural peoples such as the Goths began to migrate westwards – or because the climate did not change but the economic and political mechanisms for dealing with risk and uncertainty began to fail.[24] The prevailing modern tendency to study the history of late antiquity in terms of long-term changes through the fourth and fifth centuries, rather than focusing on isolated events such as the deposition of Romulus Augustulus in 476 CE, may be seen as part of the legacy of Braudel.

Demography, diet and disease

One reason why Braudel's history is so static may be that he focuses primarily on 'geographical frameworks' rather than 'biological realities' or 'spiritual constraints'. His account is built around the physical geography of the Mediterranean, its mountains, valleys, rivers, seasons; physical structures that have indeed remained more or less stable for long periods of time.[25] A focus on the biological components of *la longue durée* offers a different perspective. For example, nutritional studies suggest ways of developing Braudel's insight that the everyday diet of the population may affect the destiny of a culture. Everyone needs to eat, but that need can be met in innumerable different ways. Nutritionists can offer a proper evaluation of the quality of different dietary regimes and the consequences of malnutrition or vitamin deficiencies for a person's ability to function properly – and hence their ability to work, fight, reproduce and otherwise support the creation of 'civilisation'.[26] Many modern studies of food are concerned with more than the purely physiological aspects of calorie intake and nutrition but focus on issues such as availability and 'entitlement', the politics of distribution and the cultural meaning of different foodstuffs – all of which immediately suggest lines of research into antiquity. Given the limitations of a pre-industrial economy, few Greeks or Romans could take food for granted; it is at least plausible that for most of them it was more important, both physically and culturally, than politics or war.

The basic nutritional needs of the human body are more or less a biological constant. Whether or not they are met may depend on economics, politics or climate, while how they are met is a cultural matter; changes in any of these fields – in agricultural productivity, in state policies on food supply, in people's tastes – will have widespread consequences. So too will any change in the numbers of people producing food and needing to be fed.

> It should be obvious that if we have no conception of the numbers of peoples about whom we write and read we cannot envisage them in their concrete reality. What does a statement about the Romans mean if we do not know roughly how many Romans there were? Without such knowledge even politics and war cannot be understood. For instance, a description of Roman political institutions in the third century BC could only be misleading if we did not know that the citizen body was so numerous and scattered that in the absence of the representative principle the democratic features which they seem to manifest were bound to be illusory in practice.[27]

How many people could Attica or Italy support? What might this tell us about the efficiency of ancient agriculture – did ancient farmers always leave half their land fallow every year, or is there evidence of more intensive cultivation – and, if so, is there evidence that overpopulation led to the exhaustion of the land? What proportion of the Athenian citizen population were actually able to attend the Assembly and participate in political decisions? What was the level of Roman military recruitment proportionate to the total population?

Demography is often concerned less with absolute numbers – which can only be simplistic and misleading, because populations never remain static – than with structures and processes: birth and death rates, sex ratios, the age structure of the population, the ways in which populations change over time. This may provide vital insights into the structure of the family: age at marriage of men and women, numbers of children, the role of infanticide. The Roman custom of *patria potestas*, the authority of the father over his children even when they reached adulthood, is seen in a different light when one considers how unlikely it was that many Roman fathers would live long enough to exercise such authority. Similarly, the apparent dominance of the old aristocratic families in the Senate, and their reluctance to admit 'new men', is transformed by the evidence that the senatorial class was unable to reproduce itself in sufficient numbers to fill all the vacancies and so was wholly dependent on recruiting new members from the lower orders.[28] The complex interaction of human reproductive biology, social custom, nutrition and disease, among other things, that determines the structure of the population has implications for virtually every aspect of life, in antiquity as today.

Modern studies of nutrition, disease, demography and the like highlight the importance of human biology for human history. However, the main result of some of the attempts at applying these insights to antiquity has been to reveal quite how little we know about such important aspects of ancient life. On the subject of food, for example, virtually all the sources focus on elite consumption, or the diets of special groups such as soldiers or agricultural slaves, not on the consumption of the masses.

> Malnutrition has of course been studied extensively by biological and social scientists, especially in connection with contemporary developing countries. Historians who are unaware of their findings are in danger of harbouring overoptimistic assumptions

regarding the health and nutritional status of populations in antiquity and other pre-industrial societies. Among students of the ancient world, such assumptions are usually associated with a positive evaluation of the 'Mediterranean diet', one, however, which characteristically avoids the issue of availability, across the social spectrum, of an adequate supply of food-energy and necessary nutrients, and which leaves out of consideration deficiency diseases, although they certainly existed and significantly undermined the health of the population. Such accounts, in other words, pass over the phenomenon of malnutrition in all its aspects.[29]

The 'Mediterranean diet' outlined in the ancient literary sources is fine – if you receive enough of it, including all the supplementary foodstuffs as well as the basic bread and oil. The sources present us with an ideal diet, not actual consumption; but it is only when they are interrogated through comparisons with historical and contemporary material that we realise their limitations, and can start to look for alternative sources of information such as the analysis of skeletons for signs of deficiency diseases and nutritional stress.

We do not have the volume or the quality of information that is available for early modern and, in particular, for modern societies. At the very least, we can use the work of nutritionists, developmental economists and physical anthropologists to ask pertinent questions of the ancient evidence. But the comparative evidence also helps us establish some probabilities. We can, for example, hypothesise that the groups most vulnerable to malnutrition were the same in ancient societies as in developing countries today.[30]

Studies of health in antiquity are faced with the fact that ancient medical writers understood disease in an entirely different way, as the consequence of an imbalance of humours within the body, and so their recording of symptoms is quite different from that of modern medicine.[31] The underlying assumption of most studies is that our knowledge of diseases offers a way of reading these sources critically, concentrating on the symptoms that we consider to be diagnostic, so that we can tentatively identify the pathogens concerned. Of course, medical science also tells us that pathogenic organisms can mutate; new diseases are crossing over from other species all the time, and old diseases can mysteriously disappear.[32] The Great Plague at Athens has been variously identified as bubonic plague, measles and smallpox; it is at least possible that it was something unknown to modern medicine. Scholars therefore prefer to draw on a wide range of evidence, preferably physical, rather than relying wholly on the testimony of the literary sources.[33] Likewise, ancient impressions of the weather are best supplemented with, or even replaced by, archaeological evidence for temperature changes and rainfall such as the analysis of tree rings, ice cores and pollen samples.

Ancient writings on food and health are generally assumed to offer some sort of reflection of reality, even if, from the modern scientific perspective, they get it wrong (the alternative view is that, in an important sense, micro-organisms did not actually exist until Pasteur 'discovered' them; ancient diseases *were* caused by an imbalance of humours, because that is how they were experienced).[34] In the field of demography, there is a greater problem in reconciling the sources with modern understanding. As there are no ancient parish registers of births and deaths, many historians have turned to tombstone evidence, which often includes the age of the deceased and other useful information; demography suggests the sorts of questions that can be asked of material that was never intended for such uses. However, sometimes the demographic structures reconstructed from this evidence seem to be out of step with what we would expect. The classic example is the relatively small number of commemorations of those who died in infancy; in other pre-industrial populations, infant mortality was as high as 50%. Is this evidence that the Romans were far healthier than other pre-modern societies, and in demographic terms almost modern, or is it a sign that the evidence is unreliable – perhaps most Romans simply did not bother putting up tombstones for young children?

> It seems to me that the burden of proof is firmly on those who wish to assert that the Roman population in general had a lower mortality than other pre-industrial populations with similar technical achievements or towns; they must show that there were present in the Roman Empire factors which could have led to a general diminution of mortality.[35]

Hopkins takes the strong line that the ancient evidence is simply unreliable; it reflects social practices and beliefs, not demographic reality. Comparative evidence on pre-industrial populations, and especially the 'model life tables' developed to show the structures of different sorts of populations, tell us what the Roman population *must* have been like. His scepticism extends even to evidence that fits expectations:

> If we rejected evidence which does not conform to the hypothesis on the ground that it does not conform (e.g. the underrepresentation of infant mortality), we cannot usefully accept evidence which confirms the hypothesis merely because it confirms it.[36]

Other historians have been less eager to reject all ancient evidence. If it suggests that ancient life expectancy at birth was in the mid-30s, rather than 20–25 as Hopkins assumes, why can this not be correct? Hopkins's recourse to comparative evidence is based on the prior assumption that the appropriate comparisons for antiquity are underdeveloped societies with high levels of mortality and low life expectancy. If one trusts the evidence, however, it suggests that a different comparison would be more appropriate.

This problem is exemplified in the debate about the population history of Italy in the late Republic.[37] The most straightforward reading of the sources suggests that the free population grew from roughly 4.5 to 10 million; however, this seems incompatible with the historical accounts of the crisis of the Italian peasantry in this period, and so the evidence has been reinterpreted to show the population falling from 4.5 to 4 million by the time of Augustus, a decline that can be attributed to the effects of constant warfare and the displacement of peasants to make way for slave labour into the countryside.[38] This 'low' estimate has been dominant since Brunt's 1971 study of the Roman population and underpins most historical accounts of the period; if the 'high' figure were accepted, history – political history, not just economic and social – would have to be rewritten. Neither interpretation can be proved beyond doubt on the basis of the literary evidence, and so the proponents of each have turned to comparative arguments. Once again, however, it depends on prior assumptions about the ancient world, which determine what is felt to be the most appropriate comparison. The 'high' figure implies that Roman Italy was more densely populated than nineteenth-century Italy: is this grounds for rejecting it, because pre-industrial technology was not adequate to support so many people, or grounds for taking a more positive view of the efficiency of Italian agriculture? The rate of population increase seems implausibly high if Italy is compared with early modern Europe, but similar rates are known from the nineteenth-century United States. In other words, comparative evidence and modern scientific knowledge can suggest what *might* have been possible, but they cannot say how things *must* have been.

Ecology

It can be frustrating, and even disconcerting, to realise how little we know about something so basic and yet so important as average life expectancy or the population of Italy; each estimate implies an entirely different picture of the nature of the ancient world. Our ignorance is exposed, but at least we now know that we need to ask such questions, supplementing the views of the ancient sources (or replacing them altogether) with a sense of what was going on beyond their perception, at the microscopic level (nutrition, disease) or at the grand level of population dynamics. The final approach to be discussed in this chapter demands an even more radical shift of perspective, away from an anthropocentric concentration on human affairs.

Ecology 'is concerned with the relations between plants and animals and their non-living environments, and in particular with the exchanges of energy which result in the population dynamics of different species'.[39] Humans are involved in these relations, as part of the 'ecosystem', but it is only subjective prejudice to regard them automatically as the most important part and to present everything from their point of view. We should think about disease from the perspective of the various micro-organisms struggling to survive and reproduce, responding to changes in their environment by adapting to new hosts or changing their mode of transmission (for example, tuberculosis begins as a disease in cattle, passes to humans through contaminated food or water and then changes to being carried on water droplets in the breath).[40] The history of agriculture is less about the ingenuity of humans in breeding new varieties of food crop and more about the adaptive strategies of wheat, discarding defences such as tough husks in favour of qualities such as larger grain size that encourage humans to protect it from predatory herbivores and competing plants.[41]

Humans are not written out of this story altogether, but they are seen in terms of their ongoing relationships with other species, rather than plants and animals simply existing as objects for human exploitation or as the 'background' to human activities. The driving force of change is not human will but nature; as Darwin put it, 'nature gives successive variations: man adds them up in certain directions useful to him.'[42] Modern ecological studies stress that ecosystems are constantly changing as minor variations in the environment give a temporary advantage to one species or another; humans, too, have to adapt.

Humans too are part of the earth's ecosystems, whether or not they are always conscious of this fact and its implications. All plants and animals tend to modify the environment as they compete and co-operate with others to survive and flourish. In their relationship to the ecosystem, two factors distinguish humans from all other animals. First, they are the only species capable of endangering and even destroying the ecosystems on which they depend for their existence. Second, humans are the only species to have spread into every terrestrial ecosystem and then, through the use of technology, to have dominated them.[43]

Ecology does not simply suggest new ways of looking at the ancient evidence; it raises important – and disturbing – questions about the way that we conceive of our world and the way that we write our history.

The American ecologist Paul Sears describes ecology as a 'subversive' subject because it challenges many of the presumptions of modern civilization, for example that modern technology puts mankind beyond the reach of nature, or that continuous economic growth in the future is in fact desirable or even possible. This assumption underlies the economic policies of both capitalist and communist governments, but it is inherently unlikely, unless the process of controlled nuclear fusion is mastered at some time in the future. The study of historical ecology may be justified on the grounds that the roots of many current problems lie in the past, which may help to instil an appreciation that what is done today may have far-reaching consequences for our descendants . . . The concerns of ecology are in fact fundamental to understanding the course of history in general (and so the present) and ancient history in particular, irrespective of whether any particular phenomenon of the distant past has any practical consequences for the present or future.[44]

How we should respond to this new picture of the world is a controversial subject. Some writers insist on the moral neutrality of ecology; like other sciences, it simply shows how things are, rather than having anything to say about how they should be. Ecologists should study the interaction of species, without making moral judgements about the success of one particular species. One of the lessons of historical ecology is that we should be wary of assuming that one particular state is 'natural' and needs to be preserved: scientifically, there is no such thing as a 'natural' landscape or 'natural' distribution of species. 'Wilderness' is as much an artificial creation, a subjective human construct, as a city or a theme park. Change, destruction and even extinction are inherent in nature.

> The view that humans have had almost entirely negative impacts on nature – widespread among environmental historians, historical geographers, ecologists and environmentalists – paradoxically perpetuates the old Western stereotypes of humanity as active, dominating, and separate from a nature that is passive and static. A view more in tune with late twentieth-century empirical data and current ecological theory would emphasize that relationships between humans and nature are interactive and embedded within a kaleidoscopic environment in which little or nothing is permanent.[45]

The alternative perspective is that it is impossible to study such topics without paying attention to the consequences of the domination of one particular species.

> Planetary history has been fundamentally environmental history. It has been the story of a long shifting away from direct and local interaction with the earth, as the defining context of daily life, to dealing with it more indirectly and globally, through the impersonal mediation of powerful centralised political institutions, elaborate technologies, and complicated economic structures. Some will insist that there have been significant gains in that shift and strong, compelling reasons for making it. True enough, but all the same the transformation did not come without costs, ecological as well as social, and a large part of the new planetary history must entail calculating those costs and determining who or what paid them and why.[46]

   Viewing history in the long term, on a planetary scale, may engender humility or triumphalism. The one view can easily decline into the guilty denunciation of *any* human activity and the repudiation of the gains of modernity in pursuit of an (illusory) pre-industrial or even pre-*Homo sapiens* paradise. The other easily supports a complacent acceptance of the devastation of nature in the name of progress and profit. History cannot resolve such moral differences, but clearly they will influence the way that we understand the past. Ecology is no more neutral than any other approach to history.

Chapter 4

Class and status

Society

A British prime minister once declared: 'There is no such thing as society. There are individual men and women, and there are families.'[1] Given that there is an entire academic discipline, sociology, dedicated to the study of society and its workings, this is clearly a highly polemical statement. 'Society', like 'economy' or 'democracy', is always an 'essentially contested concept'; how it should be defined and studied, and how this relates to other aspects of our lives, are matters of fierce dispute. The possible reasons for Thatcher's dismissal of its very existence offer a way into the question of how different approaches to the study of 'society' might influence our understanding of the ancient world.

The term 'society' has a range of meanings, originally focused around ideas of 'companionship' (from the Latin *socius*, meaning ally or companion). In the social sciences it is now used in two main senses. First, it is applied as a general term for a relatively large community of people or system of common life: for example, we can talk of modern society, rural society, Western society. This usage does not generally carry a great deal of analytical force; we could just as easily talk of 'modernity', 'the countryside' or 'the West', without changing our meaning. However, some efforts have been made to characterise different kinds of society in this sense, drawing up a typology for comparative purposes. In these terms, classical antiquity might be labelled a 'pre-industrial', 'pre-modern' or 'traditional' society, as a means of distinguishing it from the modern; the label may be used to imply not only limited technological and economic development but also specific demographic structures, a dependence on custom and tradition rather than law as a means of regulating social affairs, a worldview formed by myth and superstition rather than by science, and so forth.

A similar approach is that developed by the sociologist Ferdinand Tönnies, distinguishing between society (*Gesellschaft*), taken to be something specifically modern, and community (*Gemeinschaft*), taken to be the dominant way of conducting relations between individuals through most of history.

> All intimate, private and exclusive living together is understood as life in *Gemeinschaft* (community). *Gesellschaft* (society) is public life – it is the world itself . . . *Gemeinschaft* is old; *Gesellschaft* is new as a name as well as a phenomenon . . . All praise of rural life has pointed out that the *Gemeinschaft* among people is stronger there and more alive; it is the lasting and genuine form of living together. In contrast to *Gemeinschaft*, *Gesellschaft* is transitory and superficial. Accordingly, *Gemeinschaft* should be understood as a living organism, *Gesellschaft* as a mechanical aggregate and artifact.[2]

This idea too is dominated by the contrast with modernity and, rather like some 'primitivist' accounts of the ancient economy, the idealisation of the pre-modern past. All these approaches tend to ignore significant differences between pre-modern societies, and to present them in primarily negative terms simply as 'not-modern'. They can serve as a reminder not to interpret antiquity unthinkingly in modern terms – being conscious of the differences, as well as the similarities, between, say, the Greek *oikos* or Roman *familia* and the modern idea of 'family' – but in general the comparison seems excessively and unhelpfully broad. This usage of 'society' is not obviously contentious; it is simply that one might prefer a different term for the same object (say, 'Britain' rather than 'British society').

The second idea of 'society' is as a particular aspect of the life of a community, the arena of social relationships and the institutions that govern them. Society in this sense is seen as a subset of society in the broader sense, distinguished from other subsets such as the economy or the state. This then offers a way of understanding human behaviour, or at least those aspects of human behaviour with a 'social character', above all those involving interaction between individuals.

> Not every type of contact of human beings has a social character; this is rather confined to cases where the actor's behaviour is meaningfully oriented to that of others. For example, a mere

collision of two cyclists may be compared to a natural event. On the other hand, their attempt to avoid hitting each other, or whatever insults, blows, or friendly discussion might follow the collision, would constitute 'social action'.[3]

One might similarly distinguish the social from the economic aspects of such a collision (the costs of injury or damage, the effects on demand for puncture repair kits, and so forth). Clearly this is an artificial, even arbitrary, distinction, an intellectual technique intended to isolate certain factors for more detailed investigation; human action is virtually always multi-faceted and determined by a number of factors.

Finley's insistence that the ancient economy can never be understood apart from ancient society and culture, which is paralleled by an insistence that ancient society can never be separated from politics, ignores the fact that this is, according to most commentators, true for the modern world as well. The interpenetration of the economic, the social, the political and the cultural is not grounds for rejecting sociological models that are developed by isolating the 'social' but simply offers a caution against the too casual application of such models to reality. However, the suggested distinction between the social and the economic is politically contentious – hence, in part, Thatcher's objection to the idea of 'society' – in so far as it posits the existence of a sphere of behaviour and values that cannot be interpreted in purely economic terms. For governments, whose decisions are governed almost entirely by 'the bottom line' of economic efficiency, this notion is potentially threatening. So too is the notion of collective social interests; Thatcher's comment was made in the context of an attack on the idea of 'entitlement', the notion that 'society' has an obligation to take care of its individual members.

The threat is aggravated, one might suspect, by the way that most sociologists approach their analysis of 'society': not by treating it as an indivisible whole but by exploring its constituent parts, the different sorts of groups, collectives and institutions through which individuals engage with one another. Thatcherite politics insisted that individuals and their families were the only real social objects; hence, that the only interests that needed to be considered were those of individual economic advantage and those of the nation. It did not recognise – or, to put it another way, sought to persuade people to discount – the existence of collective interests that transcended the individual but were smaller than the whole nation – and hence were likely to be contested with other similar groups. Such interests can be seen as divisive, threatening the unity of the nation; Thatcher's opponents, of course, argued that this was simply a means of disguising the fact that she only ever represented the interests of a particular group, not of a nation that was never in fact homogeneous or free from division. Away from such explicit politics, the vast majority of those studying 'society' would accept the need to consider the parts as well as the whole – but the arguments about the nature of those parts, and what sort of groups or collectives are most important in shaping social relationships, are equally contentious.

In studying ancient society, we face the initial problem of whether to adopt actors' or observers' categories: that is, the terms that the Greeks and Romans used to discuss their own social institutions, or the terminology developed by modern sociology. Unlike the field of economics, there was a strong ancient tradition of what we might term social analysis. Just as the terms *polis* and *res publica* cannot be translated simply as 'state', because they encompass far more, so Greek and Roman 'political philosophy', such as the *Republic* of Plato, the *Politics* of Aristotle and the *Republic* of Cicero, offers an analysis of the institutions and norms of society as a whole, not just its purely 'political' aspects. We can, therefore, offer an account of the way that the ancients saw their own societies; the question is whether we think that is sufficient. Sociologists would be in little doubt, of course: 'social life must be explained, not by the conceptions of it created by those who participate in it, but by profound causes which escape awareness'.[4] This applies to the modern world as much as to any past society; few individuals, unless they are sociologists, would think of themselves in terms of status groups or roles.

Ancient accounts in fact offer a bewildering array of categories through which to understand and subdivide ancient society. There were the formal divisions of citizens into groups based on wealth (*pentakosiomedimnoi*, *hippeis* and so on in Athens, the census classes in Rome) or on birth and/or place of residence (tribes, demes); in Rome there were also the distinctions between patrician and plebeian families and between Roman and Latin citizens, and the legal distinction between *honestiores* and *humiliores*. Other groups were not formally constituted but nevertheless clearly separated themselves from the rest of society: the *kaloikagathoi*, the old aristocracy in Athens, and the elite of Roman society, the senatorial families and the equestrians. Ancient social analysis viewed society as having been formed through the coming together of a number of households, and the *oikos* remained one of the basic building blocks of the Athenian *polis*; however, ancient analysis also tended to emphasise the division between two antagonistic groups, characterised as the rich and the poor, the few and the many. And these are simply the possible divisions among the citizen males; we also need to take account of the range of categories of non-citizens or semi-citizens – metics, *perioikoi*, *incolae*, slaves, freedmen.

Some of these categories clearly overlap (an Athenian citizen was a member of both a deme and a tribe), others are mutually exclusive or even in opposition to one another. The problem for the historian is to try to establish some sort of hierarchy: which of these categories were the most important in shaping social relationships, and so which should we use to study the workings of ancient society? How far, for example, were the census classes in Athens or Rome purely for administrative convenience, and how far did they reflect (or, indeed, promote) a sense of common interest and collective identity? Did the Athenians identify equally with their deme and their tribe? Should we focus on the formal institutions of social and political organisation, or on the more informal groups such as the aristocracy or the masses? The fact that we have to ask such questions reveals the limitations of relying purely on ancient categories to understand ancient society. We need to discover *what sort of* groups these are in order to decide on their significance; even if we prefer to use the ancient terminology rather than modern concepts, we need to relate them to modern theories on social organisation.

The argument in favour of using ancient concepts is that this is how the Greeks and Romans thought of themselves; membership of these groups formed the basis of their sense of social identity and shaped their relationships with others. To be exact, this is how the educated elite thought of themselves and the rest of society. We lack the evidence to say whether a member of the Roman *capite censi* thought of himself primarily in those terms or rather in terms of, say, his occupation, his family, his place of residence or his membership of a local cult. We certainly cannot accept without question the version of society offered by a group who were so heavily involved in the struggle for power within that society. We should note the way that Greek terms for the 'upper' classes or the 'elite' are invariably positive – the 'beautiful and good' (*kaloikagathoi*), the 'best' (*aristoi*), the 'noble' (*eugeneis*), and so forth – whereas the rest of the population are dismissed as the 'mass' (*plethos*) or the 'mob' (*ochlos*); these are not neutral terms of analysis.[5] Tacitus divides the people of Rome between the 'respectable' plebs and freedmen with ties to the aristocracy on the one hand, and the riff-raff and scum of the slave population – who were less dependent on the nobles – on the other.[6]

It is also the case that these categories are not necessarily generalisable or comparable, but are limited to a particular society or even a single city. Aristotle's definition of 'citizen', the basis of his analysis of the *polis*, is an explicit attempt at developing a general concept that may be applied to a range of concrete examples:

> There is no unanimity, no agreement as to what constitutes a citizen; it often happens that one who is a citizen in a democracy is not a citizen in an oligarchy ... Our definition of citizen is best applied in a democracy; in the other constitutions it *may* be applicable, but it need not necessarily be so ... But our own definition of a citizen can be amended so as to apply to the other constitutions also.[7]

In other words, Aristotle had to abandon the local perspective in favour of his own categories of analysis in order to develop a more general understanding of Greek society, and historians need to do the same. Even if we do not accept the argument that social action is shaped as much by unconscious factors as by conscious conceptions, at least we need to have a basis for comparing the different ways that social distinctions were conceived of in different cities. This does then create the possibility of drawing wider comparisons, making use of the range of modern ideas on how social groups function: 'socialising' their members by inculcating the norms of society, shaping individual and collective action, resolving conflicts, and so forth. These are questions that it would not be possible to ask if we relied solely on the perspective of the ancient actors.

Status

This chapter will focus on two key terms of social analysis, both of which have been used to study ancient society: status and class. The first of these is most clearly elaborated in the work of Max Weber, who developed it on the basis of data gathered from a range of historical societies, including classical antiquity.

'Status' shall mean an effective claim to social esteem in terms of positive or negative privileges; it is typically founded on (a) style of life, hence (b) formal education, which may be (α) empirical training or (β) rational instruction, and the corresponding forms of behaviour, (c) hereditary or occupational prestige. In practice, status expresses itself through (α) connubium (β) commensality, possibly (γ) monopolistic appropriation of privileged modes of acquisition or the abhorrence of certain kinds of acquisition, (δ) status conventions (traditions) of other kinds.[8]

We wish to designate as 'status situations' every typical component of the life fate of men that is determined by a specific, positive or negative, social estimation of *honour* . . . In content, status honour is normally expressed by the fact that above all else a specific *style of life* can be expected from all those who wish to belong to the circle.[9]

Society is seen to be made up of a number of 'status groups', generally arranged in a hierarchy of prestige. The number and nature of these status groups, and the precise ways in which they are marked out from one another, varies from society to society, as does the relationship between these and other sorts of groups. For example, in modern society sociologists may distinguish not only between upper, middle and lower classes but between different gradations within those groups ('upper middle', C1, C2 or C3, and so forth), marked out by such attributes as occupation, educational background, eating habits and 'conspicuous consumption' of particular goods.

These status groups are clearly differentiated from 'parties', the main form of organisation in the political sphere, although clearly high status and social esteem can often be converted into political power. Status can be understood in terms of another concept, not used by Weber but useful in this situation, namely 'social capital': something that can be accumulated, invested and converted into economic or political power. For example, consider the close relationships between parents' social class and the quality of education their children receive, and between a university education and economic power, social esteem and even political office – note the extraordinarily high percentage of Cabinet members over the last few decades who went to Oxbridge.

In earlier forms of society, there were (as far as we can tell from the available evidence) fewer distinct status groups – many modern studies follow Aristotle in setting up a simple contrast between 'mass' and 'elite' – and the distinction between society and politics was even less clear-cut.[10] It makes little sense to consider the *kaloikagathoi* or the senatorial elite as 'parties' in a modern sense, although the former claimed that they ought to be exercising political power and the latter actually did. Rather, these can be seen as status groups in societies in which social esteem was easily converted into, and frequently was a prerequisite for, political office. Membership of these groups was determined partly by birth, partly by wealth, and partly by a whole 'style of life', in Weber's phrase: dining practices, a gymnasium education, disdain for manual labour and trade, ideals such as self-sufficiency and frugality, and so forth. Such groups generally claimed to be closed, hereditary elites; in practice they depended on admitting new members, but demanded that they should conform to the unwritten rules and expectations of the group. The most eloquent spokesman for the values of the exclusive senatorial elite, our best source for the ways in which their status was expressed and policed, was Cicero, a new man from the provinces, who completely bought into their value system in order to be allowed to join.

In Rome, or at least in the Rome presented by the surviving sources, the social hierarchy was governed by the values of the elite. The freedman Trimalchio in Petronius' *Satyricon* is portrayed as desperately trying to imitate the upper class 'style of life' but getting it slightly wrong; for all his wealth, he can always be dismissed as 'vulgar' by a 'true' aristocrat. Under the Republic, political life was dominated by the elite's competition for prestige; political office was valuable in itself, of course, but also because it conferred honour on the holder and his family. Under the Principate, the rules changed, as prestige came to depend increasingly on the favour of the emperor; but 'status' remains a key term of analysis for understanding elite behaviour. In Athens, too, the political system affected the way that status operated; claims to social esteem could still be translated into political power – most of the leading orators in the assembly came from the educated elite, even if not from the oldest aristocratic families as Pericles did – but they could also become an object of suspicion if it seemed that the elite was claiming the right to rule the city, rather than the right to be leaders within the democratic system. The aristocratic style of life could be seen as 'oligarchic' and thus dangerous; orators were never sure when high social status might be considered an advantage and when a liability in the eyes of the *demos*.[11]

Further down the social scale, it is less clear how status distinctions may have operated between citizens, or how important they were. In Athens, one of the most important distinctions was between citizens and the rest.[12] Citizen status guaranteed political and legal rights and allowed the holder to own land; the privilege was jealously guarded, stripped from those found guilty of various kinds of uncitizenlike behaviour and only rarely granted to non-citizens who had done great service to the city. Rome took a different approach, granting citizenship to its allies and to many freed slaves; being a citizen brought fewer rights in a political system in which the democratic element was limited to choosing between members of the elite, but the fact that so many freedmen chose to record their acquired status on their tombstones indicates that it was still prized. The fundamental status distinction was of course between freedom and slavery – though in the later Roman Empire this seems to have become less important, as the distinction between *humiliores* and *honestiores* became starker, and the legal position of the former deteriorated.[13]

Many more examples could be given of the way that the concept of 'status' in this broad sense, in which political, legal and social status overlap and are combined, illuminates the study of the ancient world. We should, however, also note some possible problems and limitations with the use of this term. Most obviously, there are source problems; most of our impressions of the operation of status come from the perspective of the elite, whose behaviour was certainly influenced by the struggle for prestige. There is always a danger of accepting their worldview too readily, and believing that, for example, a contempt for paid manual labour was a defining feature of status distinctions throughout ancient society, rather than a concern simply of the elite – the fact that potters signed their work, and traders recorded their professions on their tombstones, suggests that they did not share that particular attitude.

It is much easier to identify a concern with social status on the part of individuals, and to explore the ways in which this was expressed in actions, relationships and literature, than it is to identify clearly defined status groups. Formal political divisions, such as the Roman census classes, do not fit the bill, because they were based solely on wealth rather than on the whole range of status indicators. It makes little sense to define senators and equestrians as separate status groups, since the boundary between them was so porous and they clearly shared a common way of life. Historians commonly refer instead to 'the Roman elite', encompassing both groups (as well as, in many cases, the municipal aristocracies of other cities within the Empire), but it has been objected that this term is too vaguely defined to be helpful.[14] Likewise, there is the question of whether 'the elite' in Athens was confined to the upper echelons of the citizen body or whether it included some wealthy non-citizens, who interacted socially with the nobility and shared in social esteem but were excluded from direct involvement in politics. Given the importance ascribed to political involvement in the ancient sources, it is tempting to include it as one of the criteria for membership of an ancient elite – but that leaves us with the question of how to categorise the wealthy and influential metics and freedmen who were heavily, if never fully, involved in ancient social affairs.

This confusion may reflect historical reality, if in fact there were no clearly defined groups governing social behaviour but only a confused and constantly shifting pattern of alliances and relationships between individuals. Alternatively, we might identify several different sets of status groups, rather than a single hierarchy: those groups in which status was determined by lifestyle ('the social elite') overlapping, but never completely identical with, those in which political activity played an important role ('the political elite', or, depending on one's view of ancient society, 'the elite' proper). This, however, risks reducing the power of the concept of status, making it descriptive rather than analytical: the idea of an assortment of 'status groups', identified by occupation or patterns of consumption, can become no more than a system of classification, rather than a means of analysing the distribution and exercise of power in society. The strength of a status-based analysis depends on how far membership of such a group is taken to influence the action of individuals and hence offers an explanation of social change – in other words, if it assumes that 'the elite' (however defined) will act collectively to maintain its position against competitors, rather than seeing that group simply in terms of a style of life to which anyone in theory might aspire.

Class

Perhaps the most significant objection to the idea of 'status groups' is not that they do not exist, or do not affect the behaviour of individuals, but that they are simply less significant than other kinds of division within society. To this may be added the thought that 'status groups' are not in principle antagonistic to one another. Individuals may feel dissatisfied with their poverty or social position, but the solution is for them to attempt to better themselves and rise to a higher status, not to try to overthrow the system.

Some set of norms governing relations of superiority and inferiority is an inherent need of every stable social system. There will be immense variation, but this is a constant point of reference. Such a patterning or ordering is the stratification system of society.[15]

There will always be social differentiation, even if not always based on noble birth or aristocratic lifestyle; compare the importance of one's place in the Party hierarchy in Soviet Russia, or of services to the *polis* in Athens, as means of acquiring social esteem in a supposedly egalitarian society. Groups differentiated simply by occupation and lifestyle should be able to co-exist happily, and any society develops mechanisms (such as the possibility of social advancement for those with talent and ambition) to regulate possible conflicts and establish consensus.

Those who regard this view of society as at best naive, and more likely a deliberate ploy to undermine opposition to the status quo, prefer a different term of analysis: class. It should be noted at the outset that this is a highly problematic term, because it is used in a number of different ways. In popular usage, it is indistinguishable from 'status group': the British 'upper middle class', for example, is defined by such attributes as professional occupation, private school and university education, a liking for Radio 4 and holiday homes in the Dordogne. In sociology, it may be used alongside 'status group' (as Weber does) to describe a stratification system based on economic criteria; for example, working class (primary industry), middle class (tradesmen and small businessmen), the landowning class and the capitalist class. However, the term is most closely associated with Marxism, in which it has a more specific and technical definition and from which it acquires many of its political overtones. Here it is offered as a clear alternative to 'status' as a mode of analysis, offering a quite different understanding of society and its operations.

The problem for the Marxist approach is that, although Marx himself used the term extensively and insisted on its importance – 'the history of all hitherto existing society is the history of class struggle' – he never provided a detailed definition of it. Much effort has therefore been expended in trying to establish exactly how Marx understood the concept. This is an important question in intellectual history; it is also important for Marxists who wish to claim the authority of the founder for their particular version.[16] Since we are concerned simply with considering what concepts may be useful in exploring ancient society, we can settle for 'a' Marxist (or Marx-inspired) definition of class rather than seeking 'the' definition – while bearing in mind that this is a word that must always be analysed carefully whenever it is encountered in a work of history, to try to establish precisely how it is being used in the particular instance.

> There are really only two ways of thinking theoretically about class: either as a structural *location* or as a social *relation*. The first and more common of these treats class as a form of 'stratification', a layer in a hierarchical structure, differentiated according to 'economic' criteria . . . In contrast to this geological model, there is a socio-historical conception of class as a relation between appropriators and producers, determined by the specific form in which, to use Marx's phrase, 'surplus labour is pumped out of the direct producers'.[17]

The 'stratification' approach falls foul of the same objections raised above about 'status', tending to be descriptive rather than analytical, and is certainly not distinctively Marxist. For that, the focus should be on the actual social relationships between different groups, rather than simply comparing their income or occupation.

> *Class* (essentially a relationship) is the collective social expression of the fact of exploitation, the way in which exploitation is embodied in a social structure. By *exploitation* I mean the appropriation of part of the product of the labour of others: in a commodity-producing society this is the appropriation of what Marx called 'surplus value'. *A class* (a particular class) is a group of persons in a community identified by their position in the whole system of social production, defined above all according to their relationship (primarily in terms of the degree of ownership or control) to the conditions of production (that is to say, the means and labour of production) and to other classes.[18]

As we might expect, the Marxist approach to 'class' is essentially materialist. Classes are defined not by their location in a hierarchy of status but by their place in the system of production; the means by which individuals support themselves and their families, and the way in which their labour contributes to the overall economic system. A clear distinction is drawn between those who own the means of production (self-sufficient peasant smallholders, capitalists) and those who have to make a living in some other way (slaves, tenants, wage labourers). Further distinctions may be based on the nature of the individual's productive activity and, above all, their relation with those in other classes; for example, the tenant farmer hands over part of the produce to the landlord in a social or economic contract, while the slave's labour power is wholly owned by the owner; the peasant works his or her own land, whereas the capitalist depends on exploiting the labour of others to make a living from property.

This definition of class, then, has a number of implications for the workings of society. First, there is a strong correlation between an individual's class and his or her level of education, diet, general state of health, living conditions, and so forth; further, access to the opportunities to improve one's social and economic position are not equally distributed throughout society, so that in fact most people remain in the class of their parents. Those with greater economic power are able to convert it into political and social power as well, to reinforce their dominant position; the state acts to enforce property rights and deal with unrest amongst the lower orders, the education system promotes the benefits of entrepreneurship and trains children to take their place as cogs in the capitalist economy, and so forth. In other words, class divisions permeate the political, social and cultural spheres as well as the economic.

Athens was a special case – the exception that proves the rule, perhaps – as political power was wielded by the masses and used to limit the power of the wealthy; politics and culture may still reflect class divisions but not the dominance of the elite and its values that is found elsewhere. Rome, and other ancient states, were dominated economically and politically by the interests of the great property owners: money brought political power, political office brought financial reward. Consider the disputes over land reform in the late Republic. The majority of senators were always opposed to such proposals, seeing them as attacks on private property in general (if not their own illegally occupied lands in particular); the few who argued for redistribution were arguably motivated by the longer term but equally self-interested belief that senatorial wealth and security would be better served by making concessions and supporting the peasant class that supplied soldiers to defend the state. It is impossible to prove such a hypothesis, but the theory that class divisions will be replicated in the political, social and cultural spheres – and that these will reflect above all the interests of the dominant class, as well as helping to sustain that dominance – offers one way of interpreting key episodes in ancient history.

The second point to note is that, in all but the simplest of societies, there is always a variety of ways of organising production, and hence there will be a number of different classes. Slaves and free labourers clearly had different positions within ancient production: neither owned the means of production, but they were exploited in quite different ways and so clearly constitute different classes.[19] Marx did argue that modern society was becoming increasingly polarised between two classes, bourgeoisie and proletariat, under the particular pressures of capitalism; but there is no suggestion that this applied to earlier societies (or, indeed, that it will ever happen completely even in the modern world). This does raise the question of how many different classes should be identified; for example, whether the position of a craftsman working alone is sufficiently distinct in economic terms from that of a craftsman working alongside his slave that they should be considered as different classes. It is, as ever, a question of the balance between sameness and difference; opponents of the concept complain that it ignores crucial differences between individuals, while its supporters argue that the basic similarity of individuals' economic position outweighs superficial differences and provides a better explanation of their place in society. It is, arguably, more useful to understand society in terms of a limited number of large classes, even if these do have internal differences and divisions, than fragmented into lots of tiny classes which differ from one another only marginally.

This leads to a third aspect of the concept of 'class': it is assumed to be an objective state, rather than a subjective identity. In other words, an individual belongs to a particular class whether or not he or she is conscious of it; status differences between individuals may serve to conceal a common class identity. This approach can be seen as arrogant – you *are* a member of the proletariat, whether you like it or not, and so you *ought* to feel exploited – and certainly depends on the assumption that the observer's analysis of the situation is more valid than the actor's superficial understanding. Those who occupy a particular position in the system of production are assumed to have common interests as a result; it is trite, but true, to say that slaves will benefit from the abolition of slavery, or low-paid casual workers from an increase in the minimum wage. Such groups would benefit if they acted collectively, but collective action (as opposed to a common position and common interests, even if not recognised as such) is not a prerequisite for the existence of a class. It should also be noted that, historically, the elite have always been far readier than the masses to recognise their class interests and to act accordingly. There is no evidence of collective action on the part of ancient slaves and, with the exception of democratic Athens, little evidence of it from the free poor; elite landowners, on the other hand, used a variety of methods to 'divide and rule' these potential enemies: selective rewards (patronage; special privileges for some slaves), avoiding keeping slaves of the same nationality together, occasional concessions and selective violence.

This is the final point to note: unlike status groups, classes are defined in direct opposition to one another. The interests of a group that controls the means of production and relies on the labour of others to exploit them can never be reconciled with the interests of those who have to sell or barter their labour power to gain access to the means of life; as Pliny suggested, not even a 'considerate and gentle' slave owner could consider himself safe.[20] Society understood in class terms is defined by conflict: 'the history of all hitherto existing societies is the history of class struggle', not necessarily in terms of open war between self-conscious classes but certainly in terms of conflicting interests and demands. These conflicts, fought out in the economic, social, political or cultural spheres, can provide a force (if not the force, as Marx argued) for change, even transformation.

For example, Rome's military successes in the middle Republic, founded on a peasant army, brought about a shift in the balance of power between landowners and peasants. The former were able to displace the latter from the land, replacing them with a more profitable system of production based on slave labour; but the ramifications of that change included the growth of the landless poor class in the city and the separation of the army from civil society. Both these factors contributed to the civil wars of the first century BCE and the political transformation that saw an oligarchy replaced with a monarchy, partly on the basis that it was better able to maintain peace and protect wealth and property rights. Similarly, the gradual disintegration of the western half of the Roman Empire in the fifth century CE can be interpreted in class terms. The landowning elite enriched themselves even to the point of undermining the state structure that had allowed them to do it, and as the state ceased to be an effective protector of property rights they turned to alternative means – entrenching themselves in their rural estates, above all – to maintain their dominance.

Politics

The most obvious objection to the concept of 'class' in the Marxist sense is that it is blatantly political, above all in its assumption that society – all society – is inevitably riven by conflict and based on the exploitation of the masses. This is not something that any Marxist would dispute.

> Whereas descriptions of ancient society in terms of some category other than class – status, for instance – are perfectly innocuous, in the sense that they will have no direct relevance to the modern world (which will of course need to be described in terms of a completely different set of statuses), an analysis of Greek and Roman society in terms of class, in the specifically Marxist sense, is indeed something *threatening*, something that speaks directly to every one of us today and insistently demands to be applied to the contemporary world.[21]

'Class' in the Marxist sense is not a neutral term of analysis. However, the Marxist claim would be that this is not grounds for rejecting it; no other term of analysis is neutral either. 'Status' may be chosen instead because it does not assume that conflict and exploitation are inherent to society – but that choice is based on the equally political assumption that it is possible to reconcile the interests of different groups and to establish consensus. It is a choice between different views of society, not between 'clean' and 'tainted' terminology. All interpretations of the past are influenced by political views; it is simply that the Marxists are open about their commitment, and about their belief that history is worth studying for what it tells us about the modern world, whereas other historians pretend to offer a value-free account of the past 'for its own sake'. Attacking the 'blood-red spectacles of Marx' is a rhetorical trick, to portray oneself as untainted by any political bias.

Of course, it is legitimate to reject the Marxist approach on the grounds that its assumptions are unconvincing – as it is to regard 'status' as, if not wrong, then at least not the whole picture, because it ignores the 'real' nature of society. Individual perceptions may be discounted, or even interpreted as a means by which class differences are concealed (the Marxist idea of 'false consciousness'), as, for example, the emphasis on the status of the free citizen, as opposed to slaves and metics, concealed the extent to which some citizens were more free and more powerful than others. Alternatively, one might argue that status distinctions actually reflected the way that people thought about themselves and hence shaped their behaviour towards one another. One approach claims to reflect the 'real' complexity of society, the other argues that it is necessary to look beyond surface complexity to the underlying structures of society to understand what is 'really' going on. Which concept is felt to be most useful may depend not just on one's interpretation of ancient society but on one's view of the world in general.

Chapter 5

A sense of identity

Sex

The development of 'social history', focusing on society as a whole and the different groups that constituted it, forced historians to consider how far their view of the past had previously been dominated by the particular perspective of the elite. We may not have the evidence to study the lower classes in as much detail as we would like, but at least we can be more aware of how far the sources are simply not telling us about a significant proportion of society. More recent theoretical developments have revealed a still larger blind spot: historians, even those using concepts such as class or status, have ignored more or less half the people who have ever lived, their role in society and their contribution to historical development. Traditional social analysis has ignored the most fundamental division in society in favour of identifying different groups of men, taking it for granted – as Western society has for centuries – that women are defined by the status and activities of their fathers and husbands, and therefore scarcely need to be discussed.

> Historians' neglect of women has been a function of their ideas about historical significance. Their categories and periodizations have been masculine by definition, for they have defined significance primarily by power, influence and visible activity in the world of political and economic affairs. Traditionally, wars and politics have always been a part of 'history', while those institutions which have affected individuals most immediately – social relationships, marriage, the family – have been outside the scope of historical enquiry. Because most women have lived outside the spheres of rewards and recognition, they have not had a history as historians have defined the term.[1]

Feminist theory, which emerged from the 'women's movement' of the 1960s, has had far-reaching effects on historical practice. It has changed our view of the past, emphasising the inadequacy or incompleteness of previous accounts, and has raised a whole series of new questions and productive lines of research. According to some commentators, it has now played its part; its ideas have been absorbed into the mainstream and it has nothing more to contribute, just as feminism in general now seems irrelevant and passé in the 'post-feminist' world it helped to create.[2] Other writers, however – and it is important to bear in mind that feminism, like most other theoretical traditions, is not a homogeneous body of doctrine but includes a range of different views and perspectives – argue that the feminist perspective remains indispensable for understanding the workings of society, past or present.

The most obvious legacy of feminism in ancient history is that 'ancient women' are now an accepted subject for historical study, like law or agriculture. It created the sense of a 'gap' or 'absence' in the historical record that inspired research into the lives of Greek and Roman women:

> This book was conceived when I asked myself what women were doing while men were active in all the areas traditionally emphasized by classical scholars. The overwhelming ancient and modern preference for political and military history, in addition to the current fascination with intellectual history, has obscured the record of those people who were excluded by sex or class from participation in the political and intellectual life of their societies.[3]

The parallel between women and the lower classes ('those . . . excluded by sex or class') is interesting, and it does seem that earlier social history provided a template for women's history in its attempts at recovering past reality.[4] Both approaches face the same problem of sources; we know far more about elite women than about those from lower classes, and even there we generally have to rely on accounts of women's behaviour written by elite males rather than direct testimony. It remains an important question whether we can gain access to the real lives of real ancient women rather than just representations and images of them. But we are at least aware that sources such as Juvenal do not provide (or even pretend to provide) an accurate picture of reality, and we can attempt to 'read against' them – unlike historians of earlier generations:

> It is easy to cite 'emancipated', or rather 'unbridled' wives, who were the products of the new conditions of Roman marriage. Some evaded the duties of maternity for fear of losing their good looks; some took a pride in being behind their husbands in no sphere of activity, and vied with them in tests of strength which their sex would have seemed to forbid; some were not content to live their lives by their husband's side, but carried on another life without him at the price of betrayals and surrenders for which they did not even trouble to blush.[5]

Carcopino's account seems thoroughly old-fashioned not only in its completely literal reading of Juvenal but in the values that inform his interpretation – the 'duty of maternity', and so forth. That is to say, his views are clearly of their time; our society has changed its attitudes towards women (or at least learnt to express them more subtly), and so our accounts of the past have also changed. 'Women' can now be found in all reputable indices for works on ancient social history (and especially in the growing field of family history) as objects of interest rather than moral condemnation.

In this respect, feminism could be said to have done its work; 'women's history' is now an accepted part of the subject (even if it is still less prestigious than political or economic history). However, feminists would argue that this is only a beginning: it is not just a matter of putting women back into the picture, filling in the gaps in the conventional account, but rather of rethinking the account completely. One thing that all feminist approaches have in common is that they regard 'woman' not just as a subject for study but as a key term of analysis, analogous to 'class' or 'status'. All women have something in common by virtue of being women, despite whatever differences there are between them in terms of status, economic position, and so forth; the structures and ideologies of society mean that they will have common interests and experiences, even if they are not fully conscious of this. All societies are divided between the two sexes, which are allotted different roles, rights, privileges and duties; historically, Western society has been patriarchal, dominated by men, with women excluded, formally or informally, from the public sphere.

This offers a new way of analysing society as a whole, in a way that is analogous to an analysis based on class: exploring the ways that political, social, economic and cultural structures and institutions reflect and reinforce male domination. This is not simply a matter of noting that women were denied the right to participate in politics, as a prelude to a conventional discussion of (male) political activity. We need to consider *why* politics was an exclusively male pursuit, what the consequences were for ancient society, and how this state of affairs was maintained. We can explore, for example, the complex of ideas about feminine lack of self-control and irrationality, developed through myths, historical anecdotes and philosophical treatises, that supported the Greeks' and Romans' belief that a woman wielding power over men was unthinkable – or, in the cases of women actually attempting to wield power, such as Cleopatra or Theodora, unnatural and potentially disastrous. The Athenians' love of depicting Amazons on vases and on the Parthenon frieze can be seen not as a purely aesthetic preference but as an expression of their wish to dominate women – and also their fear, if every citizen wife was a potential Amazon and all hopes for a legitimate heir to the *oikos* depended on their co-operation and fidelity.[6] In the economic sphere, rather than focusing exclusively on 'proper', productive work, we need to pay attention to the equally vital contribution made by women in processing and selling goods, in providing food and clothes for the labourers, in producing the next generation of workers and in providing a motive for the husband to work harder – something that was recognised by the Roman slave owner Columella, who advised his readers to give wives to their slave overseers as a way of ensuring their co-operation.

One problem with this approach is that the ancients did not view their society in these terms, and so it is impossible to establish these arguments through citation from the traditional sources; it is easy enough to pile up examples of ancient misogyny but not to demonstrate that these had a *structural* function within ancient society. That depends on whether you accept that it is appropriate and useful to interpret societies in terms of the battle between the sexes as well as, or instead of, class conflict or status differences. Like class-based analysis, feminist approaches are constantly accused of 'politicising' history, imposing a modern agenda on the past. Their response is the same, that their approach is indeed political but so too are non-feminist accounts, consciously or unconsciously. Feminists aim to expose the working of male domination in the past as a way of understanding the present; a supposedly neutral, value-free account, avoiding such loaded terms as 'patriarchy' and 'oppression', is really seeking to conceal the true nature of society. Feminist writers have been particularly conscious of the power of the past to shape present consciousness; for example, accounts of earlier forms of society based around the tribe or the household can serve to suggest that patriarchy is therefore 'the primeval, the original, hence the "natural" form of society' and hence that the 'natural' place of women in society is in the home, producing children.[7]

Feminist history not only questions the accounts that historians have given of the past, it questions their priorities and their practices. History offers a particular view of what sorts of things are 'historically significant' that does not happen to include either women's activities or the fact of male domination.

> To make a claim about the importance of women in history is necessarily to come up against the definitions of history and its agents already established as 'true' or at least as accurate reflections of what happened (or what mattered) in the past. And it is to contend with standards secured by comparisons that are never stated, by points of view that are never expressed as such. Women's history, implying as it does a modification of 'history', scrutinises the way in which the meaning of that general term has been established. It questions the relative priority given to 'his-story' as opposed to 'her-story', exposing the hierarchy implicit in many historical accounts. And, more fundamentally, it challenges both the sufficiency of any history's claim to tell a whole story and the completeness and self-presence of history's subject – universal Man.[8]

Feminism also offers the basis for a critique of the 'discipline' of history, the way that it is organised at university level. It argues that the sex of the historian, whether student or professor, will almost always make a difference. As elsewhere in contemporary society, the history profession favours males while proclaiming equality of opportunity and treatment; it favours them not through deliberate discrimination but through the institutional structure of the subject and the ways in which it works in practice. This may be seen, for example, in the qualities that are usually valued in seminar discussions (male students seem to relish the adversarial cut and thrust of debate), in the way that student work is assessed (the skills required to do well in unseen examinations are most often associated with males), in the award of research grants and appointments to jobs, in the impact of maternity leave on academic careers, in the small number of female professors. Feminism also raises the question of whether the style in which history is generally written, which claims to be neutral and transparent, is in fact recognisably 'masculine'.[9] If so, a woman historian is then faced with the choice between ventriloquism – adopting a male voice (and perhaps not being conscious of the fact that she has had to suppress her own voice) – and being marginalised within the discipline for failing to conform to its unwritten rules. Historians are not supposed to question their own profession to such an extent; failure to do so does of course benefit one particular group . . .

Gender

One of the main problems for feminist approaches to ancient history is that of the sources: in most cases their only option is to try to 'read between the lines' of male accounts, to try to gain access to the reality that, it is assumed, they reflect and distort – an approach that is all too open to the accusation that the historian is 'imposing' her prejudices on the material. Another objection, which has been raised by both women and men, is that feminism tends to make sweeping generalisations about 'women', ignoring crucial differences in their capabilities and experiences – precisely as in the last paragraph's statements about discriminatory teaching methods. There is evidence to suggest that an excessive reliance on unseen examinations may disadvantage a significant number of female students but by no means all of them.

In recent years, partly in response to such concerns and partly in response to new developments in other areas of social theory, research in this area has tended to shift its focus from 'sex' to 'gender':

> Women's history has to define its subject-matter as the history of conceptions of gender (i.e. of 'men' and 'women' as social, not natural, beings) and of the social relationships and experiences to which gender ideologies are tied.[10]

'Sex' is biological, determined by the physiological differences between men and women. Feminism has long recognised that

Eric S. suggests theory determines what counts as data.

'anatomy is not destiny', that discrimination against women is not in fact justified on the grounds of actual physical differences – in other words, that patriarchy is not 'natural' or inevitable.[11] Therefore, 'sex' is limited as a tool of social analysis; we need to focus on the way that sexual difference is interpreted and used within the social system.

> Gender is the social organization of sexual difference. But this does not mean that gender reflects or implements fixed and natural physical differences between women and men; rather gender is the knowledge that establishes meaning for bodily differences.[12]

A gender-based analysis focuses not on the categories of male and female but of 'masculine' and feminine', the cultural and ideological constructs that, in a given society, tell us what it means (or is supposed to mean) to be male or female. It broadens the analysis to cover society as a whole, not just the female half of it, and aims to deconstruct the apparent binary opposition, recognising that ideas of masculinity and femininity are almost always intertwined and mutually dependent. The feminine may be defined in terms of the absence of (allegedly) masculine characteristics, such as reason and courage, or in terms of opposition (passive–active, soft–hard, weak–strong, and so forth). The label is not applied only to females; it can also be applied to male behaviour that does not conform to social norms, such as being the passive partner in homosexual intercourse. We can understand some of the criticisms of a figure such as Nero in terms of his deviation from Roman expectations of proper masculine behaviour – while bearing in mind that we cannot be sure whether he did actually behave like that and was condemned for it, or whether accusations of deviance were the easiest way of portraying him as a bad ruler.[13] Either way, notions of gender, especially as regards sexual behaviour, played an important role in Roman political discourse.

The point that is constantly stressed is that gender is a cultural construction, not a natural fact. Human biology may be a constant, but its meaning varies widely across time and space.

> If sex were simply a natural fact, we could never write its history ... But sex is not, except in a trivial and uninteresting sense, a natural fact. Anthropologists, historians, and other students of

culture (rather than of nature) are sharply aware that almost any imaginable configuration of pleasure can be institutionalized as conventional and perceived by its participants as natural. Indeed, what 'natural' means in many such contexts is precisely 'conventional' and 'proper'.[14]

All human societies have developed norms of sexual behaviour, unwritten rules and expectations of what is 'proper', which they justify on the grounds that they are 'natural' (often reinforcing this by invoking divine authority: homosexuality as *sin*). However, the content of these norms varies enormously; historical study reveals how far our systems of morality are simply *our* systems, rather than universally valid truths, and that has obvious political implications. The idea of 'Greek love', the acceptability of same-sex relationships among the Athenians and their idealisation in poetry and philosophy, has played a role in debates about homosexuality, offering for some 'a high antique precedent for their outlawed practices'.[15] The ancient evidence undermines the assumptions on which modern prejudice is based:

> Classical authors allow themselves just as many allusions to homosexuality as they do to any other ribald topic. There is no difference between Greek and Latin writers, and the love that tends to be called Greek might equally be called Roman. Should we believe that the Romans learnt it from the Greeks, who taught them so much else? If the answer is yes, one might infer that homosexuality is such a rare perversion that one people can only have picked it up through another's bad example. If, on the other hand, it appears that pederasty was indigenous in Rome, the astonishing thing is not that a society should practise pederasty, but that it should not practise it. What needs explanation is not Roman tolerance but contemporary intolerance.[16]

In his study of ancient sexuality, David Halperin goes further along this 'cultural relativist' route, arguing that not only our moral judgements but even our categories of analysis are historically situated.

> Even the relevant features of a sexual object in classical Athens were not so much determined by a physical typology of sexes as by the social articulation of power. Sexual partners came

in two significantly different kinds – not male and female but 'active' and 'passive', dominant and submissive. That is why the currently fashionable distinction between homosexuality and heterosexuality (and, similarly, between 'homosexuals' and 'heterosexuals' as individual types) had no meaning for the classical Athenians. There were not, so far as they knew, two different modes of 'sexuality', two differently structured psychosexual states or modes of affective orientation, corresponding to the sameness or difference of the anatomical sexes of the persons engaged in a sexual act; there was, rather, but a single form of sexual experience in which all free adult males shared – making due allowance for variations in individual taste, as one might for individual palates.[17]

The very idea of categorising certain sorts of human sexual behaviour as 'homosexuality' is modern, dating from the mid-nineteenth century – when it was developed specifically as a means of stigmatising that behaviour as deviant, and of marking out 'homosexuals' as a threat to society, in need of punishment or cure.

This approach is heavily influenced by the work of the French theorist Michel Foucault, and his ideas on the relationship between knowledge and power.

Each society has its regime of truth, its 'general politics' of truth: that is, the types of discourse which it accepts and makes function as true; the mechanisms and instances which enable one to distinguish 'true' and 'false' statements; the means by which each is sanctioned; and the techniques and procedures accorded value in the acquisition of truth; the status of those who are charged with saying what counts as true.[18]

Ideas of gender and sexuality are intended to regulate the social order; not only the unwritten rules and expectations of traditional morality, but the supposedly objective accounts of medicine and social science, are used to establish a monolithic idea of 'normality' and to discipline and control those who deviate from it.

To return to sex and the discourses of truth that have taken charge of it, the question that we must address, then, is not: Given a specific state structure, how and why is it that power needs to establish a knowledge of sex? Neither is the question:

What over-all domination was secured by the concern, evidenced since the eighteenth century, to produce true discourses on sex? Nor is it: What law presided over both the regularity of sexual behaviour and the conformity of what was said about it? It is rather: In a specific type of discourse on sex, in a specific form of extortion of truth, appearing historically and in specific places (around the child's body, apropos of women's sex, in connection with practices restricting births, and so on), what were the most immediate, the most local power relations at work? How did they make possible these kinds of discourses, and conversely, how were these discourses used to support power relations?[19]

Foucault's approach may be termed 'anti-essentialising'; just as there is no universal standard of 'normal' sexual behaviour applicable to all historical societies, neither is there a naturally given, fixed 'normality' within a single society – except in so far as people can be persuaded to think that there is and adjust their behaviour accordingly. 'Masculinity' is not a stable identity founded on a physical reality, but a role, a performance, something that is constantly shifting and negotiated. It depends partly on the approach of the actor, but also on the judgement of the audience; thus, to take an extreme example, the *Übermensch* masculinity of Arnold Schwarzenegger can, from one point of view, appear astonishingly camp. A key theme in Latin love elegy is the exploration of the boundaries between masculine and feminine, the 'deconstruction' of conventional roles and expectations.[20] This approach may be extended to cover other aspects of social identity that are founded on implicit norms of behaviour. Rich Athenians brought before the courts had to persuade the jury to accept their status as loyal citizens; they were faced with the problem that there was no single correct way of doing this, and any particular act – spending money on equipping triremes, for example – might be interpreted as praiseworthy generosity towards the *polis* or as reprehensible arrogance and flaunting of wealth. Roman politicians and emperors were in the same position, always judged in moral terms but never according to a fixed, non-negotiable moral standard. The emperor attempted to play the role of an emperor, but he did not always succeed in winning over the audience to his interpretation of the part.

Further down the social scale, we can see Roman freedmen choosing to claim their legal status as a key part of their social identity and to flaunt it on their tombstones, whereas their freeborn descendants are almost invisible in the epigraphic record. In a certain context – in the law courts, for example – a particular identity might be imposed, as the system dealt with people according to its own categories (the Roman practice of classifying most citizens as *humiliores*, and dealing with them more harshly than *honestiores*, is an obvious example). Elsewhere, an individual might choose to present him- or herself in terms of legal status, family background, occupation, religious affiliation, leisure interests or anything else, shifting between possible identities in different social situations. By implication, therefore, no category of social analysis – status, class, gender – is sufficient on its own; it simply emphasises one aspect of a multi-faceted identity, and thereby runs the risk of reducing complex human behaviour to a single 'essence'.

This creates a problem for other theoretical approaches to the study of society; Foucault not only criticises the sorts of labels used by institutions and powerful individuals to regulate the rest of society, but he rejects *any* attempt at analysing society in terms of fixed categories. The idea that one can talk about 'women' or 'the proletariat' as groups that exist in reality, rather than roles that can be adopted or discarded, is seen as another essentialising discourse, another way of exercising domination over others – even if the aim of such an analysis is actually to liberate people from domination.[21] Those who want to discuss patriarchy or class exploitation as a real system of oppression can do so only by resorting to the same essentialist arguments as their opponents, insisting that women do have collective interests by virtue of being women, just as the spokesmen for 'traditional values' insist that women are intended to stay at home and raise children by virtue of being women. Foucault's argument can be attacked on the grounds that it undermines the basis for political action and thus serves to perpetuate oppression and exploitation; it is at best anarchistic, opposed to any sort of system of power and domination while acknowledging that power and domination are inherent in all social relations, and at worst quietistic.

> We should not confuse respect for the plurality of human experience and social struggles with a complete dissolution of historical causality, where there is nothing but diversity, difference and contingency, no unifying structures, no logic of process, no capitalism and therefore no negation of it, no universal project of human emancipation.[22]

But such an attack rests on precisely the assumption that Foucault rejects, that there is an objective basis for talking about oppression even if the people concerned do not see themselves as oppressed. The alternative is to accept the instability and relativity of all our concepts and categories and yet insist on their usefulness in practice: 'to acknowledge the partiality of one's story and still tell it with authority and conviction.'[23]

Ethnicity

There has been a similar move from biology to culture, with similar criticisms of 'essentialist' approaches, in the study of what used to be termed 'race' and might now be called 'ethnicity' – it is significant that in this field there is nothing remotely resembling a neutral term of analysis that does not come with copious theoretical baggage. In the nineteenth and early twentieth centuries, the key word was 'race'. Differences between peoples – most obviously, between white Europeans and the non-white inhabitants of the regions that they were conquering and settling – were attributed to biology, whereas previously they had been seen in broadly cultural terms. Typologies of races were developed; observable physical differences were assumed to point to differences in reasoning capacity and social behaviour. Inevitably, the typology was understood in terms of a hierarchy, with white Europeans at the top (and, depending on the writer, some Europeans placed higher than others) and a succession of progressively 'less developed' non-white races below. Ancient Greek ethnography, including its emphasis on geographical determinism, and the Greeks' sense of absolute superiority to 'barbarians' were reinterpreted in biological terms; ancient ideas such as Aristotle's doctrine of 'natural slavery', the inherent inability of some races to reason properly or control themselves, were brought in as intellectual support for European racism.

> Their Aegean cradle-land, with its peculiar physique, and its intimate relations with other Mediterranean coastlands, neighbouring sections of the Mountain-zone, and neighbouring annexes of the Eurasian steppe, has been for long the recipient of inhabitants from all the three primary breeds of the White Race of mankind. But it also lies sufficiently aloof and self-contained to impose its peculiar geographical controls on each and all, selecting the strains best fitted for acclimatization. As a physical

variety of man, a Greek type is always emerging in Greek lands, and during a long interval of quiescence from the eleventh to the seventh centuries BC, did actually establish itself by elimination of unconformable, uncongenial traits. From mongrel ancestry, the Greek people of classical times had come to consist of closely related types, approximately thoroughbred.[24]

The loss of Greek independence to Rome and the (generally agreed) degenerate state of the modern inhabitants of Greece were explained by the fact that Alexander's conquests had diffused the Greek race across a wide area and encouraged interbreeding with inferior races: the classical type was thus replaced with 'numerous mongrel descendants'. Similar perspectives were offered on the fall of the Roman Empire:

> What lay behind and constantly reacted upon all such causes of Rome's disintegration was, after all, to a considerable extent, the fact that the people who built Rome had given way to a different race. The lack of energy and enterprise, the failure of foresight and common sense, the weakening of moral and political stamina, all were concomitant with the gradual diminution of the stock which, during the earlier days, had displayed these qualities.[25]

The influence of 'scientific racism' on ancient history may serve as a warning of the dangers of adopting fashionable theories. The ultimate consequences of such a worldview – the enslavement of millions of non-Europeans, the slaughter of millions more in the United States, Africa and Asia, the Nazi attempt at exterminating 'inferior races' – are now well known, and have served to discredit such theories, or at least discourage their promotion in public.[26] In recent years 'race' has been abandoned almost completely as a term of analysis and replaced with 'ethnicity': the social and cultural elaboration of biological difference, the way in which differences are given meaning – or, in some cases, invented altogether.

> The problem with the nineteenth-century treatment of Greek ethnic groups was that its racial model entailed a view of biologically determined, static and monolithic categories whose boundaries were impermeable – indeed, elements of this doctrine still prevail in some current works on Greek history

which apply the term 'race' to the Dorians or Ionians ... The ethnic group is a *social construction* rather than an objective and inherently determined category. Genetic, linguistic, religious or common cultural factors cannot act as an objective and universal definition of an ethnic group. They are instead *indicia*, or the operational sets of distinguishing attributes which tend to be associated with ethnic groups once the socially determined *criteria* have been created and set in place.[27]

Ethnicity is important not because biological differences actually determine human behaviour but because a sense of ethnic identity can influence behaviour; 'race' may not really exist, but 'racism' certainly does.

This is a way of understanding how the ancients viewed their world, and, once we abandon the assumption that they must have conceptualised racial difference in exactly the same way that we do, it suggests a range of areas for further research. For example, there is the question of pan-Hellenism (a kind of Greek nationalism), an idea energetically promoted by various writers (normally in the face of an external threat such as Macedonia), on the basis of shared language and cultural and religious traditions, but counterbalanced by the equally long tradition of political fragmentation and fierce independence.[28] Nationalism in any period is really just an idea: the question is how many people accept the idea and allow it to influence their actions, 'imagining' themselves to be members of a particular community.[29] We can also compare the Greek sense of their difference from other, inferior cultures with the Roman willingness to offer citizenship to conquered peoples and former slaves – an approach which, at least by the time of Juvenal, seems to have led to a debate between those who regarded true Roman identity as a matter of birth and those who saw it in cultural terms, as something that could be acquired.[30] Ideas of ethnicity jostled with other ideas about social identity. We can explore the different ways in which a sense of identity was articulated and inculcated: in myths (Athenian autocthony or the Roman story of Romulus offering asylum to escaped slaves and criminals), in civic ceremonies and monuments, in literature and philosophy, in political institutions.

Once again, this approach to ancient history has political overtones and implications. A view of ethnicity as a cultural construct emphasises that it is not 'natural', and so neither is discrimination on ethnic grounds; the delusions and deceptions of racism are exposed. On the other hand, the phenomenon of 'ethnic cleansing' in the former Yugoslavia highlights the fact that what matters is how individuals and groups interpret the phenomenon of difference; in cultural terms, the differences between Serbs, Croats and Bosnians were often quite minimal, but the *idea* of an absolute distinction proved far more powerful.[31] This example also emphasises that ethnicity intersects and combines with other sorts of divisions, political, social and economic; the conflicts in Bosnia and Kosovo were also about differences in political and economic power, even if they were expressed in ethnic terms. We should note the importance of history in these debates; accounts of the Battle of Kosovo in 1389 were offered to justify Serb claims to the region. Ancient history can become embroiled in such arguments: the apparently academic question of whether the Macedonians under Philip were 'Greeks' is implicated in debates about the relationship between the former Yugoslav province of Macedonia and the Greek province of the same name.[32] A marginally less contentious example is Turkey's proposed entry into the European Union: does its incorporation into the classical world qualify it as 'European', even if it was subsequently separated by religion and culture? The idea of Europe itself owes much to antiquity – note how often monetary union is presented, positively or negatively, as a revival of the unity of the Roman Empire.

However, there is a wider issue for ancient history and classical studies in general: the suggestion that they are at heart racist subjects, founded on the assumption of European exceptionalism and superiority, with the aim of studying the origins of that superiority in the ancient world (or, to put it another way, of appropriating Greek civilisation as the basis for their own foundation myth). Why do we study ancient Greece and Rome, and not Egypt or Carthage, if not because we think they are (i) more important and (ii) more closely related to us? We may not hold such beliefs consciously, but they are built into the fabric of the subject; we are still working within the legacy of nineteenth-century racism.

The paradigm of 'races' that were intrinsically unequal in physical and mental endowment was applied to all human studies, but especially to history. It was now considered undesirable, if not disastrous, for races to mix. To be creative, a civilization needed to be 'racially pure'. Thus it became increasingly intolerable that Greece – which was seen by the Romantics not merely as the epitome of Europe but also as its pure childhood – could be the result of the mixture of native Europeans and colonizing Africans and Semites.[33]

Martin Bernal's critique of nineteenth-century classical scholarship has generally been well received. His further argument that Greek culture was in fact lifted almost entirely from the Egyptians – note the brilliantly provocative title of his book *Black Athena* – has been more extensively criticised on a number of grounds, not least his very literal reading of Herodotus and his view of 'cultural influence' as a straightforward, one-way process.[34] Regardless of the validity of his approach, however, he has raised some important questions about the underlying assumptions of ancient historians; as he suggests, 'it will be necessary not only to rethink the fundamental bases of "Western Civilization" but also to recognise the penetration of racism and "continental chauvinism" into all our historiography.'[35]

It cannot be disputed that ancient history has at times been influenced by racist ideas, and that it has been deployed to legitimise European conquests, enslavement, the destruction of local cultures in the name of 'civilisation', and so forth. We need to be aware that elements of this may still lurk in darker recesses of the subject, in the way in which we frame research questions (for example, evaluating the ancient economy purely in terms of Western development, so that anything not modern must be 'primitive') and in the assumptions that influence our interpretations. On the other hand, there is a real 'classical tradition' (a subject in its own right, of course), a history of people in Europe reading about and responding to the ancient world – and often using it as a means of criticising their own society, as Adam Smith condemned slavery and Marx and Engels attacked Western imperialism, not just legitimising European power.[36] The danger is to assume that the influences on the history of Europe were *only* classical, that the ancient world can only be understood in terms of the subsequent development of Europe, or that the classical heritage is exclusively European property.

Chapter 6

Myth and reason

Culture

'Culture,' Raymond Williams has suggested, 'is one of the two or three most complicated words in the English language.'[1] It has an enormous range of meanings and overtones and is used as a technical term in several different academic disciplines – with quite different definitions. In popular usage, the word is most often used to refer to the field of creative activity: literature, art and music, though in recent decades its scope has been broadened to include 'popular' culture as well as what is now labelled 'high' or 'elite' culture. In archaeology, the term primarily refers to particular material assemblages, the distinctive combination of forms, motifs and types of artefact that can be used to distinguish between different groups both over time and over space. In the relatively new field of 'cultural studies' it is applied to the entire symbolic system of a society, encompassing not only 'high' and 'low' culture as normally understood but advertising, sport, fashion, pornography – indeed, anything can be understood in terms of its cultural 'meaning'. 'Culture' can come to mean everything, and hence virtually nothing, except for vague and tendentious comparisons of 'Western' and 'Oriental' cultures. One might try to isolate one 'proper' or conventional meaning of the term, as the archaeologists do; on the other hand, 'the complex of senses indicates a complex argument about the relations between general human development and a particular way of life, and between both and the works and practices of art and intelligence'.[2] Debates about the relation between the material and the ideal and their respective influences on the production of 'meaning' within a society are only circumvented, not resolved, by narrowing the range of reference of the term.

'Culture' is introduced at this point partly as a warning; it is one of those words that must be carefully interrogated whenever it appears in a historical account, to determine how it is being used and what sorts of assumptions lie behind it. However, for all its vagueness and complexity, it does offer one way of characterising the subject of this chapter: 'theories of culture'. The phrase is intended to encompass all the different aspects of how the Greeks and Romans thought, and thought about their world: covering not just the highest products of their intelligence and creativity (the history of ideas, of science, of philosophy, and so forth) but the conceptions and assumptions that shaped the lives of the mass of the population, including such topics as religion and myth and the thought processes that underlie those conceptions.

This is an extremely broad topic, and one that overlaps with many of the subjects considered already. For example, a society's conception of sexual difference can be considered as part of its 'culture', and certainly many of the theories discussed here, if accepted as persuasive, have implications for our understanding of ancient gender relations. The process is not necessarily one-way, as theories contest one another's claims to be 'fundamental'; this chapter should be read against earlier ones, and vice versa. Sociobiology argues that sexual discrimination is founded on biological difference; feminists might respond that a patriarchal society naturally produces a sexist biology. Marxists claim that culture in general 'reflects' the underlying structures of production; Freudians might note instead the way that aspects of production – the capitalist drive to accumulate, for example – can be understood in psychological terms, a persistent survival of the 'anal' stage in libidinal development, in which the infant obtains pleasure by 'hoarding' its faeces – while Marxism's denunciation of capitalism merely expresses latent hostility towards the tyrannical father-figure.

This is of course to caricature some complex theories; even the more extensive discussions below can provide only very basic introductions, highlighting a few key ideas. First, however, we should consider some issues that are common to all attempts at exploring ancient thought. Most obviously, there is the problem of sources. However much we wish to consider the 'thought-world' of antiquity as a whole, we tend to have to rely on the accounts of the educated elite. It is, at least in this respect, easier to study, say, the history of ancient science than the history of ancient ideas of nature; the risk in attempting to do the latter is that we take the abstract and intellectual views of Aristotle and Lucretius *as* the 'ancient idea of nature' rather than as a part of it. Studies of Greek myth often have to draw not on traditional stories told and retold across generations but on highly polished literary and artistic versions of them, shaped by an individual's creative imagination for quite different purposes. Modern interpretations of ancient religion suggest that it was focused on practice and ritual rather than belief; we have at least learnt not to evaluate it in terms of our (largely Christian) assumptions about religion, but we have little direct evidence for what it actually meant for its practitioners. Ancient sources speculate about the origins of traditional rituals, which in many cases they no longer understood, and offer abstract philosophical speculation on the nature of the divine; we are left to try to infer, often using comparative anthropological evidence, the possible meanings of ancient religious practices and objects for their devotees.

This leads on to the second problem: how to determine the plausibility of our interpretations. We cannot study directly the actual processes of ancient thought, only their products. We cannot prove what was going through a Roman's mind when he dedicated a terracotta model of a foot at the temple of Diana at Nemi: we just have the foot and a range of theories about the possible meaning of such a practice. Modern theories of mind remain highly controversial for the same reason: they are unverifiable and in many cases directly contradict our own sense of how our minds work. There remains a wide gap between, on the one hand, empirical data about sequences of electrical impulses in different parts of the brain, the effects of brain damage on memories and skills and the effects of different drugs on moods and emotions and, on the other, a proper understanding of how people think and behave. At least the physiological approach can point to the existence of some relation between the biochemical workings of the brain and a person's emotional state; theories that try to study the content and meaning of thoughts and feelings can point to the limitations of the pharmaceutical approach to mental illness, but cannot offer empirical evidence to support their own interpretations. It remains a matter of plausibility: which theories seem to fit our own experiences and understanding, somehow balancing the sense that there are significant regularities in human behaviour with our own conviction of our freedom from biological determination.

There is then a further question of whether modern theories can be applied to other cultures: did the ancients think like us? The default position tends to be an unthinking assumption that they did, allowing us to interpret their behaviour in our terms – though, in the case of a votive offering, modern responses might vary from regarding it as a perfectly normal act of devotion to seeing it as an outmoded superstition or a psychological defence mechanism. In some accounts, the fifth century BCE is regarded as the moment when 'they' became like 'us', with the triumph of reason (*nomos*) over myth and the consequent invention of philosophy, science, history, and so forth. Indeed, the Greeks might be seen as almost unnaturally rational, determined (as in the case of Socrates) to subject all of human life to the merciless gaze of reason.[3]

> Some years ago I was in the British Museum looking at the Parthenon sculptures when a young man came up to me and said with a worried air, 'I know it's an awful thing to confess, but this Greek stuff doesn't move me one bit.' I said that was very interesting: could he define at all the reasons for his lack of response? He reflected for a minute or two. Then he said, 'Well, it's all so terribly *rational*, if you know what I mean.'[4]

This encounter spurred Dodds to explore the role of the 'irrational' in Greek thought, since this view of the Greeks as being like us (or more so) depends not only on focusing exclusively on the products of elite culture but also on ignoring the extent to which the non-modern, the mythical and the alien permeated ancient culture, even those aspects that seem most familiar and analogous to our own.

In emphasising difference, however, we are faced with different questions. Is there a single measure of rationality by which we can judge ancient thought, estimating its degree of primitiveness or development? This is often the assumption in discussions of ancient 'economic rationality', and one might evaluate ancient science in terms of the degree to which its practices resemble 'proper' science and its theories uncover the 'reality' of the world. Or, are there different 'reasons', different ways of viewing the world, that are equally consistent and effective and that we need to take equally seriously? Discussing the triumph of the Copernican view over those who believed that the earth was the centre of the solar system, Thomas Kuhn argued that 'if these out-of-date beliefs are to be called myths, then myths can be produced by the same sorts of methods and held for the same sorts of reasons that now lead to scientific knowledge.'[5]

Was myth simply a rather inadequate makeshift for science and social science, or are the scientific theories that purport to explain the workings of the human mind no more than modern myths, just another way of making sense of the world?

The unconscious

Probably the best-known 'scientific' approach is Freudian psycho-analysis – though its status as 'science', rather than (as its critics allege) mysticism or ideology, is controversial. There is no ignoring the influence of Freud's ideas, albeit largely in the fields of literary and cultural studies and 'agony aunt' pages rather than medicine. Key elements of his theories, such as 'repression' and 'transference', have entered general use and become 'the dominant idiom for the discussion of the human personality and of human relations'; perhaps this success accounts for the violence of some of the criticisms levelled against psychoanalysis.[6]

> Freud made no substantial intellectual discoveries. He was the creator of a complex pseudo-science which should be recognised as one of the great follies of Western civilisation. In creating his particular pseudo-science, Freud developed an autocratic, anti-empirical intellectual style which has contributed im-measurably to the intellectual ills of our own era. His original theoretical system, his habits of thought and his entire attitude to scientific research are so far removed from any responsible method of inquiry that no intellectual approach basing itself upon these is likely to endure. Still less is it likely to solve the enigma of human nature which Freud himself believed he had within his grasp.[7]

The basic problem for psychoanalysis is the same as for any at-tempt at studying human thought processes: we cannot gain direct access to what is going on in someone's mind, but have to rely on what they tell us – and one key precept of Freud's theory is that people are not in fact conscious of everything that goes on in their own minds, so we cannot accept what they tell us at face value. Psychoanalysis offers a hypothesis about the underlying determi-nants of human behaviour that cannot be proved or disproved but only judged more or less plausible – but, as Freud himself admitted, since the theory offers a new and radical interpretation of human behaviour, it is almost bound to be judged implausible.

> I will show you how the whole trend of your previous education and all your habits of thought are inevitably bound to make you into opponents of psychoanalysis, and how much you would have to overcome in yourselves in order to get the better of this instinctive opposition.[8]

Furthermore, psychoanalytical treatment, depending as it does on persuading the patient to talk about the most intimate details of his or her mental life, must be carried out in private; it cannot be observed but only experienced, or read about if the analyst publishes the (suitably anonymised) case history – 'in the strictest sense of the word, it is only by hearsay that you will get to know psychoanalysis.'[9] However, there is one instance in which the issues of privacy do not apply:

> One learns psychoanalysis on oneself, by studying one's own personality ... There are a whole number of very common and generally familiar mental phenomena which, after a little instruction in technique, can be made the subject of analysis upon oneself. In that way one acquires the desired sense of conviction of the reality of the processes described by analysis and of the correctness of its views.[10]

Freud offers a range of examples intended to indicate the existence of the 'unconscious', an area of the mind to which we do not have direct access; he highlights the 'Freudian slip' in which an unconscious or hidden thought is expressed by accident – the businessman who opens a meeting by declaring it closed, or the disappointed lover who thereafter can never remember his rival's name although he meets him regularly. We are thus compelled to admit that we may have wishes and feelings of which we are not wholly aware and which may be completely opposed to our conscious thoughts and intentions. Freud then builds on this idea: the unconscious in fact contains all the desires and thoughts that have been 'repressed', expunged from our conscious mind because we cannot admit that we have such feelings. Above all, these desires are sexual, since this is one of the most basic instincts in humans and because society establishes strict rules about what sorts of sexual desires are acceptable; above all, the sexual desires that are repressed are those that we had towards the parent of the opposite sex (while also feeling hostility and rivalry towards the same-sex parent), since this is for most people the primary relationship in their formative years, while incestuous desires are the most strictly prohibited.

Being totally honest with oneself is a good exercise. A single idea of general value dawned on me. I have found, in my own case too, [the phenomenon of] being in love with my mother and jealous of my father, and I now consider it a universal event in early childhood.[11]

Such desires can never be admitted, even to ourselves; they *must* be repressed. However, repression is never wholly successful. The unconscious is constantly seeking to express itself; it can do so in a disguised form through dreams and slips of the tongue, but if the conflict between the suppressed emotions and the conscious mind becomes too great it results in neurosis and mental illness. Psychoanalysis aims to relieve the conflict by helping the patient to recognise the problem, to uncover and come to terms with the feelings that have been repressed; as the cliché has it, 'tell me about your father'. A complete cure is impossible; all people are always more or less neurotic, since we all have desires that cannot be expressed. The hope is that self-understanding will, in time, at least relieve some of the more distressing symptoms.

The success of psychoanalysis as therapy is not the issue here; rather, we need to consider whether Freud's ideas offer a productive way of understanding aspects of ancient thought. They claim to be universally valid, applicable to all human beings; we would therefore expect to find the same patterns of repression and neurosis in historical societies. The content of the unconscious – *what* is repressed – might perhaps vary, as different cultures have different ideas of acceptable and unacceptable desires. Freud, however, tended to emphasise the universality of prohibitions against incest and patricide: both ancient Greeks and modern Europeans, if not all human beings, had 'Oedipus complexes'.

There are three main ways in which Freud's ideas might be applied to antiquity. First, one might attempt to analyse ancient individuals as a means of understanding their actions and motivation: for example, how far was Nero's erratic behaviour as emperor related to his complicated relationship with his mother? Full-blown

Freudian accounts are in fact rare, but the more general assumption that childhood relationships and experiences form the personality of the adult is common in biographies of ancient rulers. The most obvious problem here is one of evidence. Psychoanalysis normally relies on hours of conversation with the patient about their memories and feelings, not on second-hand accounts from historians with axes to grind. Some information about the childhoods of such figures is recorded in the sources; however, incidents seem to be chosen because they reveal the subject's inner character (which ancient biography tends to assume is more or less fixed from birth), rather than because they were critical points in the *formation* of the personality. Ancient ideas of the significance of dreams were quite different from the Freudian interpretation, and so the sorts of information that gets recorded in biographies or in the records of ancient dream analysis can support only the most unsubtle of psychoanalytical interpretations. Overall, the main effect of a pseudo-Freudian approach is to make ancient individuals seem more like us (or more like modern celebrities), childhood traumas and all. This approach may 'humanise' the past, and is certainly popular, but it is debatable whether it tells us much about antiquity.

The second use of Freud's ideas is as a way of analysing 'cultural products' in the broadest sense. Myths can be understood as analogous to dreams, an expression of the unconscious in a 'controlled' way: because they are 'only' stories, they allow us to admit to the existence of the desire to commit incest, patricide, cannibalism, and so forth, and to reinforce society's prohibition of such desires, without directly confronting the fact that these are actually *our* desires. We can then study myths in terms of this psychological function and also as a source of information about the contents of the ancient unconscious. Literature can be interpreted in the same way; creative artists are seen to have better access to their unconscious and to have the ability to rework it in a way that allows others to take pleasure in it and indulge *their* suppressed desires vicariously.

> A man who is a true artist . . . understands how to work over his day-dreams in such a way as to make them lose what is too personal about them and repels strangers, and to make it possible for others to share in the enjoyment of them. He understands, too, how to tone them down so that they do not easily betray their origin from proscribed sources. Furthermore, he possesses the mysterious power of shaping some particular material until

it has become a faithful image of his phantasy; and he knows, moreover, how to link so large a yield of pleasure to this representation of his unconscious phantasy that, for the time being at least, repressions are outweighed and lifted by it.[12]

The classic example is of course Sophocles' *Oedipus Rex*. Freud argued that his theories explained the power of literature, especially great literature: 'It can scarcely be owing to chance that three of the masterpieces of literature of all time – the *Oedipus Rex* of Sophocles, Shakespeare's *Hamlet* and Dostoevsky's *The Brothers Karamazov* – should all deal with the same subject, parricide.'[13]

The final aspect of Freud's ideas to consider is his general theory of society and civilisation.[14] On the one hand, he argues, humans are social animals: we need to enter into relationships in order to be able to meet at least some of our desires, and to satisfy our need for food, shelter, protection from natural dangers, and so forth. On the other hand, to be part of a society it is necessary to control one's desires and instincts: civilisation requires repression and renunciation, and the more complex a civilisation the more repression is required.

It is remarkable that, little as men are able to exist in isolation, they should nevertheless feel as a heavy burden the sacrifices which civilization expects of them in order to make a communal life possible. This civilization has to be defended against the individual, and its regulations, institutions and commands are directed to this task.[15]

One might see the performances of tragedy in Athens in these terms, as a kind of 'safety valve' for repression and a means of inculcating social norms, but the obvious example is religion. This is seen as a source of comfort and reassurance, as infantile dependence on the father (as both protector and law giver) is replaced by dependence on omnipotent father figures; the gods 'must exorcize the terrors of nature, they must reconcile men to the cruelty of fate, particularly as it is shown in death, and they must compensate them for the sufferings which a civilized life in common has imposed on them'.[16]

An obvious complaint about Freud's ideas is that they tend to ignore significant differences between cultures: all religions are interpreted in the same terms (essentially on the Judeo-Christian model, emphasising a single male deity), 'civilisation' is viewed in the most abstract terms, and all myths and literature are taken to reveal the same universal neuroses – which tend to be seen in almost entirely sexual terms. Freud himself noted some of the limitations and partiality of his approach; as he remarked of sexual symbolism, 'sometimes a cigar is just a cigar.'

> The religious ideas that have been summarized above have of course passed through a long process of development and have been adhered to in various phases by various civilizations. I have singled out one such phase, which roughly corresponds to the final form taken by our present-day white Christian civilization. It is easy to see that not all the parts of this picture tally equally well with one another, that not all the questions that press for an answer receive one, and that it is difficult to dismiss the contradiction of daily experience.[17]

Even those favourable towards psychoanalytical approaches would generally concede that they work better for some myths and some literary works than others – although of course resistance to Freud's ideas may simply reflect our unwillingness to admit to the existence of our repressed desires. Whether or not the details of his analysis are found convincing, his basic hypotheses about the role of the unconscious and of relics of the past (whether the individual or the human past) in shaping human thoughts and behaviour, and hence human culture and society, raise questions that demand serious consideration.

The human animal

Freud interprets human behaviour in terms of entities – the unconscious, the superego, and so forth – the existence of which cannot be proven but is inferred from human behaviour. The body of theory known as 'sociobiology' argues that these entities are unnecessary, and indeed wholly imaginary: human behaviour can be explained purely in terms of human biology. Humans are animals and are therefore driven by basic biological instincts and reflexes: the need for food and shelter, the urge to reproduce, the instinctive response to danger of 'fight or flight'. Humans may have developed much more sophisticated means of satisfying their needs and managing their reproduction than most animals, but the underlying motivation remains the same, the instincts that enabled the species to survive and evolve.

If the brain is a machine of ten billion nerve cells and the mind can somehow be explained as the summed activity of a finite number of chemical and electrical reactions, boundaries limit the human prospect – we are biological and our souls cannot fly free.[18]

Humans and baboons have evolved by natural selection. If you look at the way natural selection works, it seems to follow that anything that has evolved by natural selection should be selfish. Therefore we must expect that when we go and look at the behaviour of baboons, humans, and all other living creatures, we will find it to be selfish. If we find that our expectation is wrong, if we observe that human behaviour is truly altruistic, then we will be faced with something puzzling, something that needs explaining.[19]

Biological imperatives are taken to explain not just the behaviour of individuals but the form and function of social institutions; as these were developed by creatures governed by the demands of evolution, we would expect them to be in some sense 'adaptive', favouring the survival of the species – or, as Dawkins has argued, the survival of the gene, the genetic code shared by closely related individuals. Even a phenomenon such as altruism (making sacrifices, even of one's life, for the sake of another), which seems to contradict the crude 'Social Darwinist' notion of nature as a life-or-death, every-creature-for-itself struggle, can be explained as a strategy for maximising the survival chances of the gene. Other social institutions, such as sexual division of labour, the maternal instinct, male aggression and promiscuity and even conflicts between parents and children can easily be understood in these terms. Humans, like other living creatures, are in fact merely machines that ensure the genes' survival.

Sociobiology offers a radical new perspective on institutions such as marriage and the family. In ancient history, we might interpret the Athenian insistence that wives should remain in the home as the male's strategy for ensuring that he nurtures his own genetic kin rather than those of another male. Decisions on family planning are based on the balance between caring for existing children and having more children; the Roman elite's practice of limiting family size to avoid having to divide the property too many ways was unsuccessful in political terms, because many families failed to produce a male heir, but may have been more effective in ensuring the survival of particular genes by maximising the resources available to support surviving children. Of course, the use of terms such as 'strategy' should not be taken to imply conscious decision making or planning; Dawkins explicitly describes his idea of 'the selfish gene' as a metaphor, a way of understanding how different sorts of behaviour favour genetic survival. Rather, the development of such practices as the seclusion of Athenian wives may be seen as the result of natural processes: natural selection favours those individuals with a predisposition to act in a particular way (e.g. locking up their wives), and so those traits become established within the population as less successful genetic strains die out.

Sociobiology has a stronger claim than psychoanalysis to be 'scientific', since it draws on the view of evolution and natural selection that is accepted by the vast majority of professional scientists. It does present evolutionary theory as absolute truth – 'If superior creatures from space ever visit earth, the first question they will ask, in order to assess the level of our civilization, is: "Have they discovered evolution yet?"' – rather than (as philosophers of science would argue) the current best available hypothesis to explain the existing evidence.[20] The key point of contention is whether the conclusions that sociobiologists draw from their observations of the behaviour of insects and animals are valid, especially when applied to humans. Clearly it is impossible to *prove* that a particular form of behaviour – Athenian segregation of women, the courting displays of birds of paradise – is determined by the genetic imperative: the claim is rather that evolutionary biology offers the most convincing and economical explanation of the behaviour, without the need to posit metaphysical entities such as the superego.

On the face of it, this argument is more likely to convince when applied to birds of paradise than humans; we feel that we are more complex creatures, that our behaviour is determined (if not entirely then at least primarily) by conscious decisions rather than biological imperatives, and that we (unlike animals) possess 'culture'.

Between the basic drives that may be attributed to human nature and the social structures of human culture there enters a critical indeterminacy. The same human motives appear in different cultural forms, and different motives appear in the same forms. A fixed determinacy being lacking between the character of society and the human character, there can be no biological determinism. Culture is the essential condition of this freedom of the human order from emotional or motivational necessity.[21]

Scientists working within the area of 'sociobiology' – not all of them would accept the label 'sociobiologists' – disagree on the status of 'culture'. Some insist that it too can be understood in purely biological terms, as a means of increasing the survival chances of the species or the gene:

> If the brain evolved by natural selection, even the capacities to select particular aesthetic judgements and religious beliefs must have arisen by the same mechanistic process. They are either direct adaptations to past environments in which the ancestral human populations evolved or at most constructions thrown up secondarily by deeper, less visible activities that were once adaptive in this stricter, biological sense.[22]

Religion and myth might be explained in these terms, as ways of making sense of the world that aided the individual's survival – the hunter who had sacrificed to his god might be a more effective killer of deer – or as traits that survived accidentally because at least they did not *reduce* the individual's chances. The Oedipus myth reflects the biological advantages of avoiding inbreeding: 'individuals with a genetic predisposition for bond exclusion and incest avoidance contribute more genes to the next generation.'[23] Apart from the impossibility of proving or disproving such interpretations, they do not fully account for the *content* of such beliefs; just as observing how success and fame may increase a musician's opportunity for reproducing his DNA does not actually explain Mozart, or even Led Zeppelin. 'Biology, while it is an absolute necessary condition for culture, is equally and absolutely insufficient: it is completely unable to specify the cultural properties of human behaviour or their variations from one human group to another.'[24]

An interesting alternative approach is that developed by Richard Dawkins, acknowledging culture as separate from nature – though not a uniquely human attribute, since a process of cultural transmission can be observed in monkeys' use of tools and in the songs of certain birds. Culture, Dawkins argues, gives humans a special status, removing them from the absolute power of biology: 'for an understanding of the evolution of modern man, we must begin by throwing out the gene as the sole basis of our ideas on evolution.'[25] Culture gives rise to an alternative form of evolution, in which humans adapt to their environment not through physical mutation and natural selection but through the transmission and development of ideas, skills and knowledge, and in which ideas themselves evolve (compare the development of the natural sciences). Evolutionary theory offers a way of understanding this process, by focusing not on genes but on 'memes':

> Examples of memes are tunes, ideas, catch-phrases, clothes fashions, ways of making pots or building arches. Just as genes propagate themselves in the gene pool by leaping from body to body via sperms or eggs, so memes propagate themselves in the meme pool by leaping from brain to brain via a process which, in the broad sense, can be called imitation.[26]

Ideas do not literally struggle to propagate themselves (like the 'selfish gene', the 'selfish meme' is a metaphor); rather, ideas that are well adapted to their environment will naturally spread through the population.

> Consider the idea of God. We do not know how it arose in the meme pool. Probably it originated many times by independent 'mutation'. In any case, it is very old indeed. How does it replicate itself? By the spoken and written word, aided by great music and great art. Why does it have such high survival value? Remember that 'survival value' here does not mean value for a gene in a gene pool, but value for a meme in a meme pool. The question really means: What is it about the idea of a god which gives it stability and permanence in the cultural environment? The survival value of the god meme in the meme pool results from its great psychological appeal. It provides a superficially plausible answer to deep and troubling questions about existence.[27]

Memes are spread not by reproduction but by communication: 'if you contribute to the world's culture, if you have a good idea, compose a tune, invent a sparking plug, write a poem, it may live on, intact, long after your genes have dissolved in the common pool.'[28]

They do not necessarily aid the survival of the species or the gene – in some cases, as in the religious ideal of celibacy or the view of nature as something to be exploited for profit, they may be in direct opposition to it – but serve to give meaning to existence. It is not clear how far this idea offers a practical approach to the investigation of ancient culture – whether the 'meme' of memes has a high survival value – but it does attempt to reconcile the observations of the biological sciences with the concerns of anthropologists such as Sahlins, mainly by taking a more modest view of how much biology can explain.

A crucial aspect of Sahlins's concern with sociobiology is political. Observations about 'nature' have a tendency to move from 'is' to 'ought'; there is a long tradition in Western thought (a persistent, highly adaptive meme, in Dawkins's terms) of regarding the 'natural' as intrinsically correct and desirable. Thus sociobiology not only explains the origins of, say, male aggression and promiscuity in terms of biological imperatives, it thereby implies that such traits are natural and hence excusable – even that society is 'unnatural' in so far as it attempts to curb such instincts. Racial and sexual difference are legitimised by arguments from nature. Modern capitalism is shown to be the natural form of human society, since it is based on open competition and the survival of the fittest; state interference in the market, social welfare, affirmative action, and the like are all condemned as unnatural and hence doomed to fail – or, worse, tending to promote the survival of the less fit.[29]

Of course, such openly ideological statements are rarely produced by respectable scientists such as Edward O. Wilson, but his views are, at the least, not incompatible with such perspectives: 'Science may soon be in a position to investigate the very origin and meaning of human values, from which all ethical pronouncements and much of political practice flow.'[30] 'Although human progress can be achieved by intuition and force of will, only hard-won empirical knowledge of our biological nature will allow us to make optimum choices among the competing criteria of progress.'[31] This is, as Sahlins put it, a new utilitarianism, and it is based on some dubious assumptions: animal behaviour is interpreted in anthropomorphic terms – identifying 'polygamy', 'promiscuity' and 'homosexuality', for example – and the conclusions are then applied to human behaviour, thus implying that 'promiscuity' is 'natural' for males.

> [Since the seventeenth century] the competitive and acquisitive characteristics of Western man have been confounded with Nature, and the Nature thus fashioned in the human image has been in turn reapplied to the explanation of Western man. The effect of this dialectic has been to anchor the properties of human social action, as we conceive them, in Nature, and the laws of Nature in our conceptions of human social action. Human society is natural, and natural societies are curiously human.[32]

This ideological agenda is not inherent in biological approaches to human behaviour. It depends on collapsing the boundary between 'is' and 'ought', and on the assumption that, because humans are animals, they are no more than animals. In other words, it entirely discounts the role of 'culture'. Dawkins takes a different approach, with quite different political – or rather moral – implications: 'We, alone on earth, can rebel against the tyranny of the selfish replicators.'[33]

> I am not advocating a morality based in evolution. I am saying how things have evolved. I am not saying how we humans morally ought to behave. I stress this, because I know I am in danger of being misunderstood by those people, all too numerous, who cannot distinguish a statement of belief in what is the case from an advocacy of what ought to be the case. My own feeling is that a human society based simply on the gene's law of universal ruthless selfishness would be a very nasty society in which to live. But unfortunately, however much we may deplore something, it does not stop it being true. This book is mainly intended to be interesting, but if you would extract a moral from it, read it as a warning. Be warned that if you wish, as I do, to build a society in which individuals co-operate generously and unselfishly towards a common good, you can expect little help from biological nature. Let us try to *teach* generosity and altruism, because we are born selfish.[34]

Structures

One key element in defining what is 'special' about humans is language; it may not be unique to humans, but certainly all humans have an intrinsic ability to communicate, to use and understand language. Therefore, since human culture is dependent on language – or, indeed, is constituted by language – it makes sense to study it from the perspective of our understanding of how language works. This is the approach of the 'structuralism' most closely associated with the French anthropologist Claude Lévi-Strauss, which was an important influence on a generation of French ancient historians and mythographers.

'Structuralism' – once again, the label is resisted by many scholars working in this tradition – begins with modern linguistic theory, the rules and regularities that govern the use of any language even though its users are quite unaware of them. In the early twentieth century, Ferdinand de Saussure had developed the theory that language can be seen as a system of signification, in which individual signs (words, letters) have meaning only in relation to other signs.[35] Linguistic signs are arbitrary (there is nothing inherent in a fish that means it must be called a 'fish' rather than a 'poisson' or a 'hatstand'); they have meaning only as part of a wider system of signification, in relation to other words (so that, in English, the label 'fish' is conventionally applied to any vertebrate that lives in water and breathes through gills but is contrasted with amphibians). 'Day' has meaning only in relation to the balancing concept of 'night', 'spring' has meaning only within the arbitrary system of dividing the year into four seasons, and so forth. These 'systems of signification' may be languages such as English or French, or they may be smaller subsets; as, for example, 'class' has a particular meaning in the context of Marxism.

This is the basic idea that Lévi-Strauss and others applied to culture: meaning is not inherent in things, but it is attributed to them by virtue of their place in a wider scheme of signification. Put another way, things can never be understood in isolation. These 'things' can be marriage customs, eating habits, social structures, myths, rituals, literature; since human thought is structured by language, so its products replicate those structures. For example, the colour red has no intrinsic meaning; it is simply a colour. In different contexts, however, different meanings are attributed to it: a football strip, a military uniform, a pool on the floor, a stain on a sheet, the colour of someone's face, a traffic light. These meanings can overlap and blur into one another; thus the concept of 'woman', defined as the negative of 'man', comes to be associated with the negatives of things that are associated with 'man' – passive rather than active, weak rather than strong, frivolous rather than serious – and concepts such as frivolity come to be associated with the feminine.

The focus of most structuralist analysis is on the relationships between different concepts or practices that establish their significance. Thus the meaning of a red traffic light is determined by its place in a sequence of red – amber and red – green – amber – red. Concepts may be related to one another through association and analogy (male – hairy – violent, red – blood – stop – danger), or through opposition and contrast (white–black; good–evil), or in more complicated ways. By analogy with 'linguistic triangles', which establish the relationships between different sounds in terms of pitch and loudness, Lévi-Strauss identified the 'culinary triangle', the three points of which are 'raw', 'cooked' and 'rotten'. Foods are classified according to the degree of transformation from their original form and the balance between 'nature' and 'culture' (a key polarity in structuralist analysis): cooked food has been transformed through culture, rotten food has been transformed naturally. Any given food can be located somewhere on this triangle: oysters at the 'raw' apex, mature Stilton cheese at the 'rotten' point, and vegetarian sausages, in which the ingredients are not only cooked but deliberately disguised, at the third corner. At the same time, food may be judged in terms of its balance between 'too much' and 'not enough': Stilton or wine can continue the process of natural transformation for too long and become inedible; uncooked chicken is too raw; many modern foods are felt to be overprocessed, too far removed from their natural origins. None of this is intrinsic to the object, but depends on the particular system of signification; sushi might be classed as 'raw' in the West but 'cooked' in Japan (in the sense that it has been transformed through the cultural process of careful preparation). Even whether a particular object is to be considered a 'foodstuff' is culturally relative; dog would be excluded from the culinary triangle altogether in the West, but it is a delicacy in Korea.

Lévi-Strauss sees unconscious categories, far from being irrational or merely functional, as having so to speak an immanent rationality. The code is unconscious – and rational. Consequently, nothing is more natural than his seeing in the phonological system of structural linguistics the most comprehensive, transparent and universal model of that unconscious reason which underlies all social phenomena, whether we are dealing with kinship systems or mythological inventions.[36]

These ideas can certainly be applied to the study of ancient diets: the set of meanings and associations around the 'Mediterranean triad' of wheat, vines and olives (civilisation versus savagery, for a start), the associations of meat eating (not least with barbarian herdsmen rather than civilised farmers), the Pythagorean taboo against eating broad beans.[37] Other areas of ancient life can be similarly examined: marriage customs, religious rituals, gladiatorial games. Indeed, Lévi-Strauss emphasises that the different structures of meaning (sometimes termed 'codes') within a culture overlap, intersect and reinforce one another; thus, at least in theory, the social hierarchy might be elucidated through a study of eating habits, as much as eating habits need to be considered in the context of social structure (the more obvious procedure in the eyes of most historians and sociologists).[38]

Structuralist approaches have been particularly influential in the analysis of myth, which is interpreted as offering a clear insight into the contents and structures of 'the savage mind' (not, incidentally, something confined to 'savages'). Lévi-Strauss argues that the individual elements of a story (which he terms 'mythemes') have meaning only in the context of a wider system: not just the rest of the story, but all the different versions of that myth, the whole body of stories relating to a particular character, or even the entire corpus of myth within a given culture. Further, myth is seen as not just a story but a means whereby society is able to explore and resolve contradictions in its systems of signification; myth is heavily implicated in other aspects of the culture. Thus, Lévi-Strauss sees the Oedipus myth in terms of the contradiction between excessive kinship relations (Oedipus marrying his mother) and insufficient recognition of kinship relations (Oedipus killing his father). The myth, like many others (the Oresteia is an obvious example, with the conflict of loyalties between the maternal and paternal), establishes the unwritten guidelines for proper behaviour by exploring transgressions.[39]

Other myths can be seen as aetiological, or even existential, explaining the nature of the world and what is it to be human. Jean-Pierre Vernant, who acknowledges Lévi-Strauss's work as 'a turning point and a departure', develops a detailed analysis of the different levels of meaning in Hesiod's two versions of the myth of Prometheus.[40] His aim is to make out 'the organisation of the mental space (with its classificatory categories, its way of organising and codifying reality and its delineation of the different semantic fields) within which these myths were produced and in relation to which the modern interpreter can rediscover their full and complex significance'.[41]

> The logic of the story reflects the ambiguous character of the human condition in which, as a result of the 'hiding' action taken by the gods, good things and evils, whether given or not given, always turn out to be indissolubly linked together. At the same time the story defines the status of man, midway between that of the beasts and that of the gods: it is characterised by sacrifice, fire for culinary and technical operations; the woman seen both as wife and as bestial stomach, and cereal foods and agricultural labour . . . Pandora corresponds to *Bios*, the cereal food which Zeus 'hides' when he also hides his celestial fire, just as Prometheus hid the food in the form of meat in the *gaster* and the seed of stolen fire in the hollow stem. The belly of the woman, which man must plough if he wishes to have children, is like the belly of the earth that he must plough if he wishes to have wheat.[42]

As Vernant has suggested in exploring the implications of the fifth-century triumph (however partial and incomplete) of *logos* over *mythos*, 'myth, in its original form, provided answers without ever explicitly formulating the problems. When tragedy takes over the mythical traditions, it uses them to pose problems to which there are no solutions'.[43] This raises an important point; Greece and Rome were societies in which the traditional systems of meaning, the unwritten rules of behaviour and inherited views of the world, were being deliberately examined and criticised. Our sources do not offer direct access to the unconscious assumptions of ancient society but self-conscious explorations of the limitations of traditional accounts of the past (Thucydides' demolition of the Athenian story of the tyrannicides) or of conventional morality (Socrates, Euripides), carried out regardless of the social consequences of such scrutiny. In such a context, one might say that myth is not allowed to reconcile contradictions in signification in the traditional manner. That is not to say that structuralist approaches are no longer valid; even a sophisticated, self-conscious culture is still founded on language and so reflects its structures. Cartledge's exploration of the role of polarities in forming the Greek sense of identity (male not female, free not slave, human not animal, and so forth) draws on Aristotle and Thucydides as well as less intellectual sources.[44]

Lévi-Strauss's anthropology is not the only 'structuralist' approach to the study of culture; the idea was also developed in the Annales School with the notion of *mentalités*, the mental structures that, in Braudel's phrase, 'form prisons of the *langue durée*'. Braudel, of course, then ignored cultural factors almost entirely in favour of the material influences on human history. However, other Annalistes, especially the founders Bloch and Febvre, devoted time to identifying and discussing the ideas that shaped human behaviour – that defined, perhaps, the limits of what it was possible to think. Bloch's classic study of the 'king's evil', a skin disease that could, it was believed, be cured by the royal touch, was concerned to explain the persistence of an idea that must constantly have been contradicted by events (or rather by the lack of a miraculous cure).[45] His account of feudalism explored the influence of medieval ideas of the self, of time and space and of friendship and kinship in shaping the social structure.[46]

Another classic account of *mentalité* is Le Roy Ladurie's account of the Pyrenean village of Montaillou in the late thirteenth and early fourteenth centuries.

> What was it that made a citizen of Montaillou 'tick' in the period 1290–1325. What were the fundamental motivations, the centres of interest which, over and above such basic biological drives as food and sex, gave his life meaning?[47]

The study is based on the detailed records of a church inquisition, which record something close to the inhabitants' own words and allow the reconstruction of their emotional as well as the physical world.

> We have no statistics on the subject, but it may be that the people of Montaillou wept slightly more easily than we do, both in happiness and in sorrow. People cried, of course, at the prospect or reality of misfortune, or for the death of someone dear to them, in particular for the death of a child, even when it was very young. Both men and women grew pale, trembled and wept when afraid that they were about to be betrayed to the Inquisition. Among the shepherds, we see men bursting into

tears at a breach of friendship or solidarity, especially when accompanied by threats foreshadowing arrest by the Inquisitors.[48]

The Annalistes do not offer detailed guidance on how to study *mentalités*; Le Roy Ladurie can draw on an exceptionally rich source dealing with a limited case, without having to worry about the methodological and theoretical problems inherent in drawing together diverse sources to reconstruct the 'mental structures' of an entire culture – how to select and prioritise sources (is Aristotle more 'representative' of Greek ideas than Plato?), whether we assume the existence of a unified culture, and so forth. The idea of *mentalité* does still work simply as a way of thinking about the relation between cultural ideas and the individual; it can also highlight the question of cultural change, bringing in Braudel's ideas about different levels of historical time. We might contrast ephemeral intellectual fashions, which played a prominent part in individuals' day-to-day lives and consciousness, with long-lived, taken-for-granted concepts that shaped their view of the world over centuries. One example of the latter would be the idea that the world was the centre of the solar system (if not the universe), which informed scientific theories until the seventeenth century; another is the ancient belief that human society had degenerated from a Golden Age and would continue to degenerate, which, it has been argued, contributed to the ancient failure to develop technology to improve humanity's lot.[49]

In practice, however, the Annalistes tend, as much as Lévi-Strauss, to offer synchronic explorations of static structures, with limited attention to how and why structures of thought might change over time. Lévi-Strauss is extremely conscious that the cultures he studies are disappearing and becoming in a sense corrupted, partly as a result of the very process of contact and communication between cultures, the expansion of the West across the world, that underpins anthropology:

> Western Europe may have produced anthropologists precisely because it was a prey to strong feelings of remorse, which forced it to compare its image with those of different societies in the hope that they would show the same defects or would help to explain how its own defects had developed within it. But even if it is true that comparison between our society and all the rest, whether past or present, undermines the basis of our society, other societies will suffer the same fate.[50]

Cultural change in non-Western cultures can be explained by their contact with the West; change is here seen to be endogenous. It is less clear how the West became so different in the first place, unless we posit its particular features at the moment of European expansion as a natural fact or inherent tendency, already visible in Greek ethnography and Roman imperialism. This also affects our view of antiquity. In the absence of a theory of endogenous change, there is a danger either of reaching a dead end – at which we can say no more than that the Greeks and Romans are different from us – or of erasing all the differences between past and present, as we can explain our mental habits only by assuming that they must always have been there.

Cultures

Myths and other cultural practices differ enormously between cultures. The usual scholarly response to this fact has been to try to explain these differences, in terms either of a narrative of human development from primitive to modern, or of underlying principles and regularities that are expressed in different ways. Like psychoanalysis and sociobiology, structuralism assumes that cultures are at root comparable: 'even in regions distant from each other and despite the difference in their stories, these myths all teach the same lesson.'[51] Order and sense can be identified in the apparently chaotic and multifarious world of human thought.

> What Lévi-Strauss has made for himself is an infernal culture machine. It annuls history, reduces sentiment to a shadow of the intellect, and replaces the particular minds of particular savages in particular jungles with the Savage Mind immanent in us all.[52]

The anthropologist Clifford Geertz takes a quite different line on how one should approach 'cultural difference'. Like the structuralists, he views culture as a public system of signification and meaning, 'a set of control mechanisms – plans, recipes, rules, instructions (what computer engineers call "programs") – for the governing of behavior'.[53] All societies have such rules and customs, which clearly meet a human need: 'man is precisely the animal most desperately dependent upon such extragenetic, outside-the-skin control mechanisms, such cultural programs, for ordering his behaviour.'[54] However, whereas most approaches focus on the underlying principles, what is important and interesting for Geertz is the fact of variety, the fact that humans can produce so many different ways of managing sexual relations or deciding what to eat. Reducing this variety to a single set of principles denies the individualism of people and their cultures and is closely tied to a sense of cultural superiority over the 'savage' – Geertz describes himself as an 'anti-anti-relativist', committed to recognising the irreducibility of other cultural perspectives.[55]

> The major reason why anthropologists have shied away from cultural particularities when it came to a question of defining man and have taken refuge instead in bloodless universals is that, faced as they are with the enormous variation in human behavior, they are haunted by a fear of historicism, or becoming lost in a whirl of cultural relativism so convulsive as to deprive them of any fixed bearings at all.[56]

The crucial point in Geertz's analysis is that 'reductionism' is not only ethnocentric, it misses the point completely. The meaning of cultural acts is not to be found in underlying structures but in the mass of contextual detail particular to that society. The content of the codes governing diet or marriage is far more important than the fact that they share certain organising principles with similar codes in other cultures.

> Believing, with Max Weber, that man is an animal suspended in webs of significance he himself has spun, I take culture to be those webs, and the analysis of it to be therefore not an experimental science in search of law but an interpretive one in search of meaning. It is explication I am after, construing social expressions on their surface enigmatical.[57]

Geertz offers the example of two boys rapidly contracting the eyelids of their right eyes:

> In one, this is an involuntary twitch; in the other, a conspiratorial signal to a friend. The two movements are, as movements, identical . . . Yet the difference, however unphotographable, between a twitch and a wink is vast; as anyone unfortunate enough to have had the first taken for the second knows. The winker is

communicating, and indeed communicating in a quite precise and specific way . . . The winker has not done two things, contracted his eyelids and winked, while the twitcher has done only one, contracted his eyelids. Contracting your eyelids on purpose when there exists a public code in which so doing counts as a conspiratorial signal is winking. That's all there is to it: a speck of behavior, a fleck of culture, and – voilà! – a gesture.[58]

And, of course, the precise meaning of a wink can change according to context. Geertz's point is that the significance of the gesture cannot be understood if it is reduced to an 'essence' (the physical movement). To understand a cultural act, we need as much information as possible about its context, all the different codes which govern meaning; 'thick' description rather than the 'thin' analysis of structuralism. The anthropologist's task (that is, the task of anyone seeking to understand an alien culture) is to describe, to explicate and to interpret, suggesting between different practices and concepts.

> One can start anywhere in a culture's repertoire of forms and end up anywhere else. One can stay, as I have here [in his analysis of Balinese cockfighting], within a single, more or less bounded form, and circle steadily within it. One can move between forms in search of broader unities or informing contrasts. One can even compare forms from different cultures to define their character in reciprocal relief. But whatever the level at which one operates, and however intricately, the guiding principle is the same: societies, like lives, contain their own interpretations. One has only to learn how to gain access to them.[59]

Geertz's method is really an anti-method; he regards theoretical concepts as being of little use and potentially reductionist, and prefers to generalise within cases and not across them.[60] This is similar in some ways to the substantivist approach to the ancient economy, with its insistence on employing 'actors' categories' rather than imposing anachronistic (and ethnocentric) modern concepts. It raises the question of whether it is actually possible to 'translate' another culture in this way without something being lost or distorted in the process. Certainly, as Geertz admits, we are not presented with 'the culture itself' but only the anthropologist's interpretation, an imaginative fiction, which, since we can hardly repeat the fieldwork (or travel back in time to investigate ancient Athens for ourselves), we can only judge in terms of our (anachronistic) ideas and expectations.[61]

> The culture of a people is an ensemble of texts, themselves ensembles, which the anthropologist strains to read over the shoulders of those to whom they properly belong. There are enormous difficulties in such an enterprise . . . But to regard such forms as 'saying something of something', and saying it to somebody, is at least to open up the possibility of an analysis which attends to their substance rather than to reductive formulas professing to account for them.[62]

In Geertz's view, this is all that we can do, and it is sufficient; his aim is to bring a culture to life, to try to understand it as its native inhabitants do, simply to 'enlarge the universe of human discourse'. Difference is not something that needs explanation; we should study other cultures, including the past, as an end in itself. Those who seek other sorts of knowledge from the past will find that 'thick description' goes only so far without the introduction of general theoretical concepts to enable comparison across cultures. However, they should not ignore Geertz's warning that reducing the complexity of human experience to underlying principles, whether psychological, biological or linguistic, misses almost everything that is distinctive and meaningful about human behaviour and culture.

Afterword
Speaking theory

One of the aims of this book was to serve as a sort of guidebook to the world of theory, a simplified map of this complex territory, pointing out some of the most prominent landmarks as an aid to navigation. *Most of the buildings in this area of the subject were influenced by the long-standing rivalry between primitivists and modernisers, and even more modern constructions reveal traces of the characteristic styles of each camp.* Alternatively, it might be thought of as a manual for theory spotters, outlining the distinctive features and natural environment of these exotic creatures: *MARXISTS Distinctive blood-red plumage; found almost everywhere but especially in social and economic studies; harsh cry of 'Exploitation! Class Struggle!' Note: innumerable subspecies compete fiercely for territory.*

But 'theory' is not after all another world (and theoreticians are not another species). Rather, one might see individual theories as different cultures or languages, similar to our own traditional ancient history culture in some ways (since we all have sets of concepts and assumptions, rules about how to interpret evidence, ideas about what constitutes an interesting question, and so forth) and quite different in others (in the *content* of those concepts, assumptions and rules). When we encounter the inhabitants of another theoretical culture, we need to know enough to recognise that they are speaking a different language, or at least a different dialect, and to find some way of translating it into our own idiom. Of course, we could simply stay at home and read nothing that disturbs our settled worldview, or carry the same attitude abroad and marvel at the ignorance of foreigners who seem to misunderstand even when we Talk Very Loudly at them. The alternative is to recognise that 'foreign' theoretical ways may make sense in their own terms, even if we would not want to live there; learning to speak another language allows us to see and describe the world differently, and to recognise some of the blind spots and gaps in our own way of doing things.

This book can offer only a very basic introduction to some of the key concepts of these theoretical cultures – not enough to enable you to 'speak' them, but sufficient, I hope, to help you recognise when someone else is using the language. The guide to further reading will give some pointers towards more detailed introductory works; you can also follow up leads in books that are heavily influenced by a particular theory (they will generally indicate this in the introduction and suggest further bibliography; indeed, some can be quite evangelistic about their chosen approach). Finally, you can employ the usual skills of research to find relevant material in libraries, looking beyond the habitual haunts of the ancient history books. I hope that this book has given at least some indication of which theoretical languages it might be worth considering for your particular purposes. One important thing to note, given that ancient historians are usually consumers rather than producers of theory: it is always best to be a discerning consumer, comparing different approaches, even within a particular theory, to make sure that you do not go home with something past its sell-by date and unfit for consumption.

Some theories might be a more obvious choice for a topic than others, in terms of their traditional scope. I can just about imagine what a Freudian economics might look like, but I suspect that you would have to do most of the work yourself to construct it on the basis of Freud's general principles, whereas there are already existing Marxist, sociological, anthropological, feminist, sociobiological, etc. theories of economics on which you could draw. On the other hand, if you are convinced of the validity of the psychoanalytical approach to the study of human society in general, it would be worth the effort to apply it to economics. We can make use of particular bits of theories for particular problems on a pragmatic, eclectic basis, or we can adopt a theory wholesale, accepting it as a superior way of making sense of the world. 'Theory' not only suggests ways of thinking about a particular problem, it can redefine the problem and suggest completely different questions that need to be asked; it offers a new perspective, an alternative way of looking at things.

This does raise the question of how to evaluate different theories, different worldviews. Clearly, Marxists and non-Marxists, or feminists and non-feminists, see the world in quite different and incompatible ways. I am not proposing the sort of theoretical multiculturalism that implies that everyone could get along if they only talked to one another; some theoretical differences are far more irreconcilable than ethnic or religious distinctions. Successful theories make sense and offer a convincing view of the world in their own terms; they can always be criticised from the perspective of another theory, including the implicit, semiconscious theoretical assumptions of traditional ancient history. A key argument of most of the theories discussed in this book is that there is never a neutral position, never a neutral language in which to discuss such issues. Of course, most of them, including traditional ancient history, insist that *their* theory offers a true picture of reality, whereas all the others are partial and ideological.

We can insist on the absolute validity of our version and critique other accounts on that basis; we can abandon any attempt at judgement, imitating Geertz's refusal to impose a single reductive meaning on the varieties of human understanding; or we can attempt what may seem an impossible task, 'to acknowledge the partiality of one's story (indeed of all stories) and still tell it with authority and conviction.'[1] This predicament confronts any attempt at talking about the past, whether or not we speak 'theory'.

Notes

I Approaches

1 Shaw 1982, 17.
2 For discussion of the issues involved in the interpretation of historical evidence, see Morley 1999, 53–95, and Fulbrook 2002.
3 On 'keywords', with illuminating discussions of many such terms (including 'theory'), see Williams 1983.
4 See Finley 1981; 1985a, 123–40 and 191–6; 1985b, 61–6.
5 Parkins 1997.
6 Cf. Finley 1975.
7 Or, one might reject the study of individual biography altogether, as telling us nothing useful about the way that ancient society worked.
8 Finley 1981, 20.
9 Ibid.
10 Finley 1985b, 66.
11 Finley 1981, 20.
12 Finley 1985b, 61.
13 Further on the 'consumer city': Jongman 1988; Whittaker 1990; 1993; Nippel 1991.
14 Of course, these alternatives are neither mutually exclusive nor exhaustive of the possible interpretations of ancient *phalli*.
15 Morris 2002, 8–9.
16 Morris 2002, 8–9.
17 For an example of this approach, see Hopkins 1978b.
18 Braudel 1973, 373; Holton 1986.
19 See the essays by Wirth and Simmel in Sennett 1969; also Mumford 1961 and Laurence 1997.
20 Finley 1981, 7.
21 See e.g. Millett 1990; Woolf 1997; Alston 2002.
22 Cf. Eisenstadt and Shachar 1987.
23 Finley 1981, 5–6.
24 Williams 1983.
25 Abrams 1978. Cf. Morley 1996, 21–4.
26 For one usable definition, see Eisenstadt and Shachar 1987, 68–74.

27 *The Eighteenth Brumaire of Louis Bonaparte* [1852], in Marx and Engels 1968, 93.
28 Cf. Graham 1992, 17–19; Callinicos 1995, 96–121; Wood 1995, 146–78.
29 Cf. Popper 1952; 1957.
30 Spengler 1926; cf. Frank 1962; and for a modern example, Berman 2000.
31 See generally Ladyman 2002. The classic text is Kuhn 1970.
32 E.g. Dawkins 1976. Cf. Ladyman 2002, 129–61.
33 Cf. Popper 1972; 1974; Ladyman 2002, 62–92.
34 Cf. Morley 1996.
35 Burke 1980, 35.
36 Chorley and Haggett 1968, 22.
37 von Thünen, in Hall 1966, 7–8.
38 Weber 1949, 90
39 Finley 1985b, 66.
40 Whittaker 1993; Parkins 1997.
41 Finley 1985a, 194.
42 Hopkins 1978a, 11.
43 Hopkins 1978a, 1980. Hopkins's methodology is discussed in Shaw 1982.
44 Hopkins 1978a, 2, n.4.
45 Hopkins 1980, 101. On Hopkins's rhetorical approach, see Morley, forthcoming.
46 Hopkins 1978a, 19–20.
47 Millar 1977, xii–xiii.
48 Marx 1976a, 998–9.
49 Cf. Morley 1999, 117–22; and forthcoming.
50 See generally Williams 1983.
51 Finley 1981, 21–2.
52 Finley 1985b, 66.

2 Ancient and modern

1 Jean-Baptiste Say, *A Treatise on Political Economy* (1880), quoted in Morley 1998, 95.
2 Finley 1985a, 21.
3 Jones 1948, 1.
4 Karl Marx and Frederick Engels, *The Manifesto of the Communist Party* [1848], in Marx and Engels 1968, 39.
5 Nassau Senior, *Political Economy* (1854), quoted in Morley 1998, 111.
6 James Steuart, *An Inquiry into the Principles of Political Oeconomy* (1805), and J.-B. Say, *A Treatise on Political Economy* (1880), both quoted in Morley 1998, 112.
7 Marx 1976a, 719.
8 Marx 1976a, 271.
9 Letter to Henzen, quoted in Gooch 1920, 457.
10 Meyer 1922, n.38 to 'Die Sklaverei im Altertum', 169–212.
11 Meyer 1922, 89.
12 Rostovtzeff 1926, 10.

13 Frank 1927, 271.
14 Cf. D'Arms 1981.
15 On Pompeian cloth production, Moeller 1976; Jongman 1988.
16 Rostovtzeff 1957, 139.
17 Garnsey and Saller 1987, 43.
18 Hopkins 1983b, xi–xii.
19 Sahlins 1974, xi–xii.
20 Finley 1979, 13.
21 Carandini 1983, 202.
22 Greene 1993, 41.
23 Mauss 1954, 8.
24 von Reden 1995, 105.

3 The limits of the possible

1 Hegel 1988; see Singer 1983.
2 Weber 1930. General account in Käsler 1988.
3 Max Weber, *The Economic Ethic of the World Religions*, in Gerth and Mills 1948, 280.
4 Marx and Engels, *The German Ideology*, in Marx 1976b, 36–7.
5 Marx and Engels, *The German Ideology*, in Marx 1976b, 41–2.
6 Marx 1976a, 176, n.35.
7 Burke 1990; Horden and Purcell 2000, 38–9.
8 Febvre 1925, 367.
9 Braudel 1972, 20–1.
10 Braudel 1972, 21.
11 Braudel 1972, 21.
12 Braudel 1980, 34.
13 Braudel 1980, 33.
14 Burke 1980, 26.
15 Braudel 1972, 1244.
16 Braudel 1981, 27.
17 Bintliff 1991.
18 Garnsey 1988; Gallant 1991.
19 Braudel 1981, 107.
20 Braudel 1981, 161.
21 Horden and Purcell 2000, 42.
22 Hughes 1994, 199.
23 For example, Rackham 1996, Horden and Purcell 2000, 298–341.
24 On barbarian migration, Whittaker 1994, 215. Generally on changes in the later Roman Empire, Tainter 1988, Schiavone 2000.
25 Or at any rate stable in their instability, in so far as it has been argued that the Mediterranean ecology is defined by fragmentation, variation and unpredictability, 'unity in diversity': Horden and Purcell 2000, 10–25.
26 Garnsey 1999.
27 Brunt 1971, 3.
28 Hopkins 1983a.
29 Garnsey 1999, 43–4.

30 Garnsey 1999, 51.
31 Zivanovic 1982; Grmek 1989; Ranger and Slack 1992; Hope and Marshall 2000;
32 Wills 1996.
33 E.g. Sallares 2002.
34 Cf. Latour 1988.
35 Hopkins 1966/7, 264.
36 Hopkins 1966/7, 264.
37 On this topic see, among others, Brunt 1971; Lo Cascio 1994; Morley 1996, 46–50; 2001; Scheidel 2001, 52–7.
38 As in Hopkins 1978a; cf. Rathbone 1981.
39 Simmons 1993, 48.
40 Manchester 1992.
41 Sallares 1991, 333–61.
42 Darwin 1968, 90, quoted in Sallares 1991, 359.
43 Ponting 1991, 17.
44 Sallares 1991, 4.
45 Horden and Purcell 2000, 339.
46 Worster 1988, 6.

4 Class and status

1 Margaret Thatcher, in *Women's Own* magazine, 3 October 1987.
2 Tönnies 1955, 37–9.
3 Weber 1968, 23.
4 Émile Durkheim, quoted in Traugott 1978, 127.
5 Austin and Vidal-Naquet 1977, 24.
6 Tacitus, *Histories* 1.4.
7 Aristotle, *Politics* 1275a2–1275b13.
8 Weber 1968, 305–6.
9 Weber 1968, 186–7.
10 See generally Finley 1985a, 35–61.
11 Ober 1989, 335–6.
12 Cartledge 1993, 90–117.
13 Garnsey and Humfress 2001, 83–106.
14 Cf. Shaw 1982, 31.
15 Parsons 1964, 325.
16 Cf. de Ste Croix 1981, 30: 'I myself believe that there is nothing in this book which Marx himself (after some argument, perhaps!) would not have been willing to accept.'
17 Wood 1995, 76.
18 de Ste Croix 1981, 43.
19 *Contra* Finley 1985a, 49.
20 Pliny, *Epistles* 3.14.
21 de Ste Croix 1981, 45.

5 A sense of identity

1 Gordon *et al.* 1976.

2   Cf. Faludi 1991; Scott 1991, 43.
3   Pomeroy 1975, ix.
4   Cf. Scott 1991, 21–2.
5   Carcopino 1941, 104.
6   Cf. Cartledge 1993, 63–89.
7   Millett 1971, 108–9.
8   Scott 1991, 51
9   Spender 1985; Hallett and van Nortwick 1997; Barry 2002, 126–30.
10   Humphreys 1985, 42.
11   Cf. Greer 1970, 25–52.
12   Scott 1988, 2.
13   Cf. Elsner and Masters 1994; Edwards 1993.
14   Winkler 1990, 171.
15   Taplin 1989, 133–5.
16   Veyne 1985, 35.
17   Halperin 1990, 33.
18   Foucault 1980, 131.
19   Foucault 1986, 10.
20   Kennedy 1993, 24–45.
21   Butler 1992.
22   Wood 1995, 263.
23   Scott 1991, 60, see generally 42–66.
24   Myres 1930, 531–2.
25   Frank 1962, 54–5.
26   Hall 1997, 12–13.
27   Hall 1995, 8–9.
28   Cartledge 1993, 42–5; Hall 2002.
29   On 'imagined communities', see Anderson 1991. Generally on nation-alism (as a modern phenomenon), Gellner 1983.
30   Morley 2003, 153–5.
31   Glenny 1996; Denitch 1994; Judh 1997.
32   Pettifer 1999.
33   Bernal 1987, 29.
34   Cf. Lefkowitz and Rogers 1996; Berlinerblau 1999; and Bernal 2001.
35   Bernal 1987, 2.
36   See Beard and Henderson 1995.

6 Myth and reason

1   Williams 1983, 87.
2   Williams 1983, 91.
3   Cf. Nietzsche 1999, 64–75; generally, Buxton 1999
4   Dodds 1951, 1.
5   Kuhn 1970, 2. On Kuhn's account of scientific revolutions, see Ladyman 2002, 93–122.
6   The quote is from Gellner 1985.
7   Webster 1995, 438.
8   Freud 1973, 40.
9   Freud 1973, 43.

10 Freud 1973, 44.
11 Letter to Wilhelm Fliess, 15 October 1897, quoted in Storr 1989, 23.
12 Freud 1973, 423–4.
13 'Dostoevsky and parricide', in Freud 1985b, 453–4
14 Freud 1985a.
15 'The future of an illusion', in Freud 1985a, 184.
16 Freud 1985a, 197.
17 Freud 1985a, 199.
18 Wilson 1978, 1.
19 Dawkins 1976, 4.
20 Dawkins 1976, 1.
21 Sahlins 1977, 11.
22 Wilson 1978, 2; cf. Shermer 1997.
23 Wilson 1978, 38.
24 Sahlins 1977, xi.
25 Dawkins 1976, 205.
26 Dawkins 1976, 206.
27 Dawkins 1976, 207.
28 Dawkins 1976, 214.
29 See generally Sahlins 1977, 71–107.
30 Wilson 1978, 5.
31 Wilson 1978, 7.
32 Sahlins 1977, 93.
33 Dawkins 1976, 215.
34 Dawkins 1976, 3.
35 Barry 2002, 41–4.
36 Paz 1970, 11.
37 Garnsey 1999, 62–99, but also 7–11 on some of the limitations of structuralism. Also Detienne 1977, Corbier 1989.
38 Goody 1982, 14–29.
39 But see Vernant's critique of Lévi-Strauss's account of Oedipus: 1980, 226–33.
40 Vernant 1980, 233; other structuralist approaches to Greek myth and religion in Burkert 1979 and Gordon 1981.
41 Vernant 1980, 177.
42 Vernant 1980, 177.
43 Vernant 1980, 214.
44 Cartledge 1993.
45 Bloch 1973.
46 Bloch 1962.
47 Le Roy Ladurie 1980, 353.
48 Le Roy Ladurie 1980, 139.
49 Reece 1969.
50 Lévi-Strauss 1977, 443.
51 Lévi-Strauss 1972, 228.
52 Geertz 1973, 355.
53 Geertz 1973, 44.
54 Ibid.
55 Geertz 1984.

56 Geertz 1973, 43–4.
57 Geertz 1973, 5.
58 Geertz 1973, 6.
59 Geertz 1973, 453.
60 Cf. Levi 1991, 98–104.
61 Cf. Hopkins 1999.
62 Geertz 1973, 453.

Afterword

1 Scott 1991, 60.

Guide to further reading

Approaches

General historical theory: Morley 1999 offers a very basic introduction; more detailed contemporary discussions are to be found
in Fulbrook 2002, Jenkins 1991 and Berkhofer 1995. Burke 1980
focuses on the use of sociological theory in history; Burke 1991 offers
discussions of a range of different approaches to history, including
women's history, history from below and history of images. Theory
in ancient history: important chapters in Finley 1975 and 1985b,
Hopkins 1978c (a review article on Millar 1977), Cameron 1989 and
Morris 2002 (specifically on theoretical approaches to the subject of
'gain', but with some useful general observations). Theories of cities:
Holton 1986 is an excellent introduction to the various problems.
The 'consumer city' model is developed in Finley 1981 and 1985a,
and discussed and debated by innumerable historians including
Hopkins 1978b, Jongman 1988, Nippel 1991, Whittaker 1990 and
1993, Morley 1996 and Parkins 1997. For an attempt at an alternative approach to the ancient city, see Alston 2002. Hopkins's 'taxes
and trade' model is criticised by, among others, Duncan-Jones 1990
and 1994; and now see Hopkins's revised version in Scheidel and von
Reden 2002, pp.190–230.

Ancient and modern

Finley 1985a remains a key text on the ancient economy, but see
also Frederiksen 1975, Harris 1993, Morris 1994 and the papers by
Cartledge and Andreau in Scheidel and von Reden 2002 (pp.11–32
and 33–49 respectively), all of which also offer introductions to the
key issues in the 'primitivist–moderniser' debate. Political economy

and classical antiquity: Morley 1998. Formalism and substantivism: Polanyi 1944 and 1968, Cook 1966 and Hill 1986. Sahlins 1974 is a classic of substantivist anthropology; Halperin 1988 is a relatively recent discussion in economic anthropology. New approaches to the ancient economy: Mattingly and Salmon 2001, Cartledge *et al.* 2002, and papers in Scheidel and von Reden 2002. Another collection, *The Ancient Economy: Evidence and Models*, edited by Joe Manning and Ian Morris, is due for publication by Stanford University Press in the near future and promises to be interesting.

Limits of the possible

The Annales School: the key works are Braudel 1972 and 1981, along with the more theoretical papers collected in Braudel 1980 (especially 'Social science and history: *la longue durée*'); Burke 1990 provides a history and an overview; Bintliff 1991 explores the application of Braudel's ideas to archaeology, especially archaeological survey. Food: Garnsey 1988 and especially 1999 (which includes lots of suggestions for further reading), Wilkins *et al.* 1995 and Davidson 1997 (a very 'culturalist' approach to the topic). Demography: Parkin 1992 and Scheidel 2001 offer clear introductions to sources and problems. Ecology: Chapman and Reiss 1992 offers a clear introduction to the subject; more detailed studies include Begon *et al.* 1990 and Krebs 1994; see also Simmons 1993, for an introduction to issues in environmental history, and Wall 1994, for a collection of provocative writings on 'green history'. Sallares 1991 is the key attempt at applying ecological ideas to ancient history but is somewhat forbidding. Hughes 1975 and 1994 are less theoretical and much more pessimistic; Shipley and Salmon 1996 offers a range of approaches to the ancient environment. Horden and Purcell 2000 is a provocative and compendious exploration of different aspects of life in the Mediterranean, including discussions of a range of theories (including Braudel) concerned with the impact of geography and climate on the lives of its inhabitants.

Class and status

The second chapter of Finley 1985a remains a key discussion of the issues for antiquity. General discussions of class, status and stratification are legion: Crompton 1998 is a clear introduction to the issues; other interesting works include Breen and Rottman 1995,

Brennan 1997 (on Weber), Day 2001 (mainly from the literary perspective), Scott 1996 and Wood 1995. There are plenty of works on Greek or Roman social history which draw on ancient terminology: those that incorporate explicit discussion of modern terms such as class and status include: for Greece, Austin and Vidal-Naquet 1977, Ober 1989, de Ste Croix 1981, Vernant 1980, pp. 1–18, and Wood 1988; for Rome, Beard and Crawford 1985, Harris 1988, MacMullen 1974, Nicolet 1980; for a Marxist interpretation of the end of the Roman Empire, Anderson 1974.

Sex, gender and ethnicity

Greer 1970 and Millett 1971 are classic feminist texts; Beasley 1999, Evans 1995 and Tong 1989 offer introductions to the varieties of modern feminist thought. On feminist history and women's history, see Carroll 1976, Kleinberg 1988 and Scott 1988 and 1991. Pomeroy 1975 is the first study of ancient women from a feminist perspective; other works on ancient women (not all of it explicitly feminist) include Cameron and Kuhrt 1983, Clark 1989, Hawley and Levick 1995, Pomeroy 1991. On gender, see Glover and Kaplan 2000 and Jackson and Scott 2002 (a reader). On ancient gender and sexuality, see Cohen 1991, Hallett and Skinner 1997, Halperin et al. 1990, Halperin 1990 and Larmour et al. 1998. Skinner 1985 includes an essay on Foucault; see also Barker 1998 or Danaher et al. 2000. On ethnicity as a term of analysis, see Fenton 2003 and Jenkins 1997; for antiquity, Hall 1997, Jones 1997 and Malkin 2001. Black Athena: Bernal 1985 and, surveying the subsequent controversy, Lefkowitz and Rogers 1996, Berlinerblau 1999, and Bernal 2001.

Culture and mentality

See general introductions to theories of thought and consciousness in Priest 1991 and Seager 1999. Freud: Storr 1989 is a clear, concise introduction; Wollheim 1971 is rather enthusiastic; Webster 1995 is thoroughly damning; Easthope 1999 is a readable survey (particularly concerned with the implications for the study of literature). On the application of psychoanalysis to history, see Gay 1985, Horden 1985 and Stannard 1980. Sociobiology: key texts are Wilson 1975 and 1978 and Dawkins 1976; on the 'social Darwinist' background, Hawkins 1997; see also critiques in Sahlins 1977 and Rosenberg 1981; as yet these ideas have not been employed by ancient historians, although there are echoes in Sallares 1991. Structuralism: basic introductions in Leach 1970 and 1976 and Sturrock 1986; Skinner 1985 has a chapter on Lévi-Strauss; Clarke 1981 has critique; Gordon 1981 collects key essays by the French structuralist mythographers; for structuralism in archaeology, see Tilley 1990. On the Annales School and *mentalité*, see Burke 1990 and Le Goff 1985. Geertz 1973 collects his own most influential articles, which are discussed by Inglis 2000 and Moore 1997; Toner 1995 applies some of his ideas to a study of Roman leisure.

Bibliography

Abrams, P., 1978, 'Towns and economic growth: some theories and problems', in Abrams, P. and Wrigley, E.A., eds, *Towns in Societies: Essays in Economic History and Historical Sociology*, Cambridge, pp. 9–33.

Abrams, P. and Wrigley, E.A., 1978, *Towns in Societies: Essays in Economic History and Historical Sociology*, Cambridge.

Alston, R., 2002, *The City in Roman and Byzantine Egypt*, London.

Anderson, B., 1991, *Imagined Communities: Reflections on the Origin and Spread of Nationalism*, rev. edn, London.

Anderson, P., 1974, *Passages from Antiquity to Feudalism*, London.

Austin, M.M. and Vidal-Naquet, P., 1977, *Economic and Social History of Ancient Greece: An Introduction*, London.

Barker, P., 1998, *Michel Foucault: An Introduction*, Edinburgh.

Barry, P., 2002, *Beginning Theory: An Introduction to Literary and Cultural Theory*, 2nd edn, Manchester.

Beard, M. and Crawford, M., 1985, *Rome in the Late Republic*, London.

Beard, M. and Henderson, J., 1995, *Classics: A Very Short Introduction*, Oxford.

Beasley, C., 1999, *What Is Feminism? An Introduction to Feminist Theory*, London.

Begon, M., Harper, J.L. and Townsend, C.R., 1990, *Ecology: Individuals, Populations and Communities*, 2nd edn, Oxford.

Berkhofer, R.F., 1995, *Beyond the Great Story: History as Text and Discourse*, Cambridge, MA.

Berlinerblau, J., 1999, *Heresy in the University: The Black Athena Controversy and the Responsibilities of American Academics*, New Brunswick, NJ.

Berman, M., 2000, *The Twilight of American Culture*, London.

Bernal, M., 1987, *Black Athena: The Afroasiatic Roots of Classical Civilization*, Volume I: *The Fabrication of Ancient Greece, 1785–1985*, London.

—— 2001, *Black Athena Writes Back: Martin Bernal Responds to his Critics*, Durham, NC

Bintliff, J., ed., 1991, *The Annales School and Archaeology*, Leicester.

Bloch, M., 1962, *Feudal Society*, 2nd edn, London.

—— 1973, *The Royal Touch*, London.

Braudel, F., 1972, *The Mediterranean and the Mediterranean World in the Age of Philip I*, trans. S. Reynolds, London.

—— 1973, *Capitalism and Material Life, 1400–1800*, trans. M. Kochan, London.

—— 1980, *On History*, Chicago.

—— 1981, *Civilization and Capitalism, 15th–18th Century*, Volume I: *The Structures of Everyday Life: The Limits of the Possible*, rev. S. Reynolds, London.

Breen, R. and Rottman, D.B., 1995, *Class Stratification: A Comparative Perspective*, London.

Brennan, C., 1997, *Max Weber on Power and Social Stratification: An Interpretation and Critique*, Aldershot, Surrey.

Brunt, P.A., 1971, *Italian Manpower 225 BC – AD 14*, Oxford.

Burke, P., 1980, *Sociology and History*, London.

—— 1990, *The French Historical Revolution: The Annales School 1929–89*, Cambridge.

—— ed., 1991, *New Perspectives on Historical Writing*, Cambridge.

Burkert, W., 1979, *Structure and History in Greek Mythology and Ritual*, Berkeley, CA.

Butler, J., 1992, 'Imitation and gender insubordination', in Fuss, D., ed., *Inside/Out: Lesbian Theories, Gay Theories*, New York, pp. 13–31.

Buxton, R., ed., 1999, *From Myth to Reason: Studies in the Development of Greek Thought*, Oxford.

Callinicos, A., 1995, *The Revolutionary Ideas of Karl Marx*, 2nd edn, London.

Cameron, A., ed., 1989, *History as Text*, London.

Cameron, A. and Kuhrt, A., eds, 1983, *Images of Women in Antiquity*, London.

Caplan, A.L., ed., 1978, *The Sociobiology Debate*, New York.

Carandini, A., 1983, 'Columella's vineyard and the rationality of the Roman economy', *Opus* 2, 177–204.

Carcopino, J., 1941, *Everyday Life in Ancient Rome*, Harmondsworth, Middx.

Carroll, B.A., ed., *Liberating Women's History: Theoretical and Critical Essays*, Urbana, IL.

Cartledge, P., 1993, *The Greeks: A Portrait of Self and Others*, Oxford.

Cartledge, P., Cohen, E.E. and Foxhall, L., eds, 2002, *Money, Labour and Land: Approaches to the Economies of Ancient Greece*, London.

Chapman, J.L. and Reiss, M.J., 1992, *Ecology: Principles and Applications*, Cambridge.

Chorley, R.J. and Haggett, P., eds, 1968, *Socio-economic Models in Geography*, London.

Clark, G., 1989, *Women in the Ancient World*, Oxford.

Clarke, S., 1981, *Foundations of Structuralism*, Brighton.

Cohen, D., 1991, *Law, Sexuality and Society: The Enforcement of Morals in Classical Athens*, Cambridge.

Cook, S., 1966, 'The obsolete "anti-market" mentality: a critique of the substantive approach to economic anthropology', *American Anthropologist* 68, 323–45.

Corbier, M., 1989, 'The ambiguous status of meat in ancient Rome', *Food and Foodways* 3, 223–64.

Crompton, R., 1998, *Class and Stratification: An Introduction to Current Debates*, 2nd edn, Cambridge.

Danaher, G, Schirato, T and Webb, J., 2000, *Understanding Foucault*, London.

D'Arms, J.H., 1981, *Commerce and Social Standing in Ancient Rome*, Cambridge, MA.

Darwin, C., 1968, *The Origin of Species by Means of Natural Selection*, Harmondsworth, Middx.

Davidson, J., 1997, *Courtesans and Fishcakes: The Consuming Passions of Classical Athens*, London.

Dawkins, R., 1976, *The Selfish Gene*, Oxford.

Day, G., 2001, *Class*, London.

Denitch, B., 1994, *Ethnic Nationalism: The Tragic Death of Yugoslavia*, Minneapolis.

Detienne, M., 1977, *The Gardens of Adonis: Spices in Greek Mythology*, Hassocks, Surrey.

Dodds, E.R., 1951, *The Greeks and the Irrational*, Berkeley, CA.

Duncan-Jones, R.P., 1990, *Structure and Scale in the Roman Economy*, Cambridge.

—— 1994, *Money and Government in the Roman Empire*, Cambridge.

Easthope, A., 1999, *The Unconscious*, London.

Edwards, C., 1993, *The Politics of Immorality in Ancient Rome*, Cambridge.

Eisenstadt, S.N. and Shachar, A., 1987, *Society, Culture and Urbanization*, Newbury Park, CA.

Elsner, J. and Masters, J., eds, 1994, *Reflections of Nero: Culture, History and Representation*, London.

Evans, J., 1995, *Feminist Theory Today: An Introduction to Second-wave Feminism*, London.

Faludi, S., 1991, *Backlash: The Undeclared War against Women*, London.

Febvre, L., 1925, *A Geographical Introduction to History*, London.

Fenton, S., 2003, *Ethnicity*, Oxford.

Finley, M.I., 1975, 'Generalizations in ancient history', in Finley, M.I., ed., *The Use and Abuse of History*, London, pp. 60–74.

—— 1979, 'Classical Greece', in Finley, M.I., ed., *Second International Conference of Economic History, Aix-en-Provence, 1962,* Volume I: *Trade and Politics in the Ancient World*, New York, pp. 11–35.

—— 1981, 'The ancient city: from Fustel de Coulanges to Max Weber and beyond', in Shaw, B.D. and Saller, R., eds, *Economy and Society in Ancient Greece*, London, pp. 3–23.

—— 1985a, *The Ancient Economy*, 2nd edn, London.

—— 1985b, *Ancient History: Evidence and Models*, London.

Foucault, M., 1980, *Power/Knowledge: Selected Interviews and Other Writings, 1972–1977*, New York.

—— 1986, *The History of Sexuality*, Volume II: *The Use of Pleasure*, trans. R. Hurley, London.

Frank, T., 1927, *An Economic History of Rome*, 2nd edn, London.

—— 1962, 'Race mixture in the Roman empire', in D. Kagan, ed., *Decline and Fall of the Roman Empire: Why Did it Collapse?*, Boston, pp. 44–56.

Frederiksen, M., 1975, 'Theory, evidence and the ancient economy', *Journal of Roman Studies* 65, 164–71.

Freud, S., 1973, *Introductory Lectures on Psychoanalysis* (Penguin Freud Library 1), Harmondsworth, Middx.

—— 1985a, *Civilization, Society and Religion* (Penguin Freud Library 12), Harmondsworth, Middx.

—— 1985b, *Art and Literature* (Penguin Freud Library 14), Harmondsworth, Middx.

Fulbrook, M., 2002, *Historical Theory*, London.

Gallant, T.W., 1991, *Risk and Survival in Ancient Greece: Reconstructing the Rural Domestic Economy*, Cambridge.

Garnsey, P., 1988, *Famine and Food Supply in the Graeco-Roman World: Responses to Risk and Crisis*, Cambridge.

—— 1999, *Food and Society in Classical Antiquity*, Cambridge.

Garnsey, P. and Humfress, C., 2001, *The Evolution of the Late Antique World*, Cambridge.

Garnsey, P. and Saller, R., 1987, *The Roman Empire: Economy, Society, Culture*, London.

Gay, P., 1985, *Freud for Historians*, Oxford.

Geertz, C., 1973, *The Interpretation of Cultures*, New York.

—— 1984, 'Anti anti-relativism', *American Anthropologist* 86, 263–78.

Gellner, E., 1983, *Nations and Nationalism*, Oxford.

—— 1985, *The Psychoanalytical Movement, or, the Coming of Unreason*, London.

Gerth, H. and Wright Mills, C., eds, 1948, *From Max Weber: Essays in Sociology*, London.

Glenny, M., 1996, *The Fall of Yugoslavia*, 3rd edn, Harmondsworth, Middx.

Glover, D. and Caplan, C., 2000, *Genders*, London.

Gooch, G.P., 1920, *History and Historians in the Nineteenth Century*, London.

Goody, J., 1982, *Cooking, Cuisine and Class: A Study in Comparative Sociology*, Cambridge.

Gordon, A.D., Buhle, M.J. and Dye, N.S., 1976, 'The problem of women's history', in Carroll, B.A., ed., *Liberating Women's History: Theoretical and Critical Essays*, Urbana, IL, pp. 75–92.

Gordon, R.L., ed., 1981, *Myth, Religion and Society*, Cambridge.

Graham, K., 1992, *Karl Marx, Our Contemporary: Social Theory for a Post-Leninist World*, Hemel Hempstead, Herts.

Greene, K., 1993, 'The study of Roman technology: some theoretical considerations', in Scott, E., ed., *Theoretical Roman Archaeology: First Conference Proceedings, Newcastle, 24–24 March 1991*, Aldershot, Surrey, pp. 39–47.

Greer, G., 1970, *The Female Eunuch*, London.

Grmek, M.D., 1989, *Diseases in the Ancient Greek World*, Baltimore, MD.

Hall, J.M., 1995, 'Approaches to ethnicity in the early Iron Age of Greece', in Spencer, N., ed., *Time, Tradition and Society in Greek Archaeology*, London, pp. 6–17.

—— 1997, *Ethnic Identity in Greek Antiquity*, Cambridge.

—— 2002, *Hellenicity: Between Ethnicity and Culture*, Chicago.

Hall, P., ed., 1966, *Von Thünen's Isolated State*, Oxford.

Hallett, J. and van Nortwick, T., 1997, *Compromising Traditions: The Personal Voice in Classical Scholarship*, London.

Hallett, J. and Skinner, M.B., eds, 1997, *Roman Sexualities*, Princeton, NJ.

Halperin, D.M., 1990, *One Hundred Years of Homosexuality and Other Essays on Greek Love*, London.

Halperin, D.M., Winkler, J.J. and Zeitlin, F., eds, 1990, *Before Sexuality: The Construction of Erotic Experience in the Ancient Greek World*, Princeton, NJ.

Halperin, R.H., 1988, *Economies Across Cultures: Towards a Comparative Science of the Economy*, London.

Harris, W.V., 1988, 'On the applicability of the concept of class in Roman history', in Yuge, T. and Doi, M., eds, *Forms of Control and Subordination in Antiquity*, Leiden, pp. 598–610.

—— 1993, 'Between archaic and modern: some current problems in the history of the Roman economy', in Harris, W.V., ed., *The Inscribed Economy*, Ann Arbor, MI, pp. 11–29.

Hawkins, M., 1997, *Social Darwinism in European and American Thought*, Cambridge.

Hawley, R. and Levick, B., eds, 1995, *Women in Antiquity: New Assessments*, London.

Hegel, G.W.F., 1988, *Introduction to the Philosophy of History*, trans. L. Rauch, Indianapolis.

Hill, P., 1986, *Development Economics on Trial*, Cambridge.

Holton, R.J., 1986, *Cities, Capitalism and Civilization*, London.

Hope, V.M. and Marshall, E., eds, 2000, *Death and Disease in the Ancient City*, London.

Hopkins, K., 1966/7, 'On the probable age structure of the Roman population', *Population Studies* 20, 245–64.

—— 1978a, *Conquerors and Slaves: Sociological Studies in Roman History I*, Cambridge.

—— 1978b, 'Economic growth and towns in classical antiquity', in Abrams, P. and Wrigley, E.A., eds, *Towns in Societies: Essays in Economic History and Historical Sociology*, Cambridge, pp. 35–77.

—— 1978c, 'Rules of evidence', *Journal of Roman Studies* 68, 178–86.

—— 1980, 'Taxes and trade in the Roman Empire', *Journal of Roman Studies* 70, 101–25.

—— 1983a, *Death and Renewal: Sociological Studies in Roman History II*, Cambridge.

—— 1983b, 'Introduction', in Garnsey, P., Hopkins, K. and Whittaker, C.R., eds, *Trade in the Ancient Economy*, London, pp. ix–xxv.

—— 1999, *A World Full of Gods: Pagans, Jews and Christians in the Roman Empire*, London.

Horden, P., ed., 1985, *Freud and the Humanities*, London.

Horden, P. and Purcell, N., 2000, *The Corrupting Sea: A Study of Mediterranean History*, Oxford.

Hughes, J.D., 1975, *Ecology in Ancient Civilizations*, Albuquerque, NM.

—— 1994, *Pan's Travail: Environmental Problems of the Ancient Greeks and Romans*, Baltimore, MD.

Humphreys, S.C., 1985, 'What is women's history?', *History Today* 35, 42.

Inglis, F., 2000, *Clifford Geertz: Culture, Custom and Ethics*, Cambridge.

Jackson, S. and Scott, S., eds, 2002, *Gender: A Sociological Reader*, London.

Jenkins, K., 1991, *Re-thinking History*, London.

Jenkins, R., 1997, *Rethinking Ethnicity: Arguments and Explorations*, London.

Jones, A.H.M., 1948, *Ancient Economic History*, London.

Jones, S., 1997, *The Archaeology of Ethnicity: Constructing Identities in the Past and Present*, London.

Jongman, W., 1988, *The Economy and Society of Pompeii*, Amsterdam.

Judh, T., 1997, *The Serbs: History, Myth and the Destruction of Yugoslavia*, New Haven, CT.

Käsler, D., 1988, *Max Weber: An Introduction to his Life and Work*, Cambridge.

Kennedy, D.F., 1993, *The Arts of Love: Five Studies in the Discourse of Roman Love Elegy*, Cambridge.

Kleinberg, S.J., 1988, *Retrieving Women's History*, Oxford.

Krebs, C.J., 1994, *Ecology*, 4th edn, New York.

Kuhn, T., 1970, *The Structure of Scientific Revolutions*, 2nd edn, Chicago.

Ladyman, J., 2002, *Understanding Philosophy of Science*, London.

Larmour, D.H.J., Miller, P.A. and Platter, C., eds, 1998, *Rethinking Sexuality: Michel Foucault and Classical Antiquity*, Princeton, NJ.

Latour, B., 1988, *The Pasteurization of France*, Cambridge, MA.

Laurence, R., 1997, 'Writing the Roman metropolis', in Parkins, H., ed., *Roman Urbanism: Beyond the Consumer City*, London, pp. 1–20.

Le Goff, J., 1985, 'Mentalities: a history of ambiguities', in Le Goff, J. and Nora, P. eds, *Constructing the Past: Essays in Historical Methodology*, Cambridge.

Le Roy Ladurie, E., 1980, *Montaillou: Cathars and Catholics in a French Village*, Harmondsworth, Middx.

Leach, E., 1970, *Lévi-Strauss*, London.

—— 1976, *Culture and Communication: The Logic by Which Symbols Are Connected*, Cambridge.

Lefkowitz, M.R. and Rogers, G.M., 1996, *Black Athena Revisited*, Chapel Hill, NC.

Levi, G., 1991, 'On microhistory', in Burke, P., ed., *New Perspectives on Historical Writing*, Cambridge, pp. 93–113.

Lévi-Strauss, C., 1972, *The Savage Mind*, London.

—— 1977, *Tristes Tropiques*, New York.

Lo Cascio, E., 1994, 'The size of the Roman population: Beloch and the Augustan census figures', *Journal of Roman Studies* 84, 23–40.

MacMullen, R., 1974, *Roman Social Relations 50 BC to AD 284*, New Haven, CT.

Malkin, I., ed., 2001, *Ancient Perceptions of Greek Ethnicity*, Cambridge, MA.

Manchester, K., 1992, 'The palaeopathology of urban infections', in Bassett, S., ed., *Death in Towns: Urban Responses to the Dying and Dead, 100–1600*, Leicester, pp. 8–14.

Marx, K., 1976a, *Capital*, Volume I, trans. B. Fowkes, Harmondsworth, Middx.

—— 1976b, *Collected Works*, Volume V, London.

Marx, K. and Engels, F., 1968, *Selected Works in One Volume*, London.

Mattingly, D. and Salmon, J., eds, 2001, *Economies Beyond Agriculture in the Classical World*, London.

Mauss, M., 1954, *The Gift*, trans. I. Cunnison, Glencoe, Argyll.

Meyer, E., 1922, *Kleine Schriften zur Geschichtstheorie und zur wirtschaftliche und politischen Geschichte des Altertums*, Halle.

Millar, F., 1977, *The Emperor in the Roman World (31 BC – AD 337)*, London.

Millett, K., 1971, *Sexual Politics*, London.

Millett, M., 1990, *The Romanization of Britain: An Essay in Archaeological Interpretation*, Cambridge.

Moeller, W.O., 1976, *The Wool Trade of Ancient Pompeii*, Leiden.

Moore, J.D., 1997, *Visions of Culture: An Introduction to Anthropological Theories and Theorists*, Walnut Creek, CA.

Morley, N., 1996, *Metropolis and Hinterland: The City of Rome and the Italian Economy*, Cambridge.

—— 1998, 'Political economy and classical antiquity', *Journal of the History of Ideas* 26, 95–114.

—— 1999, *Writing Ancient History*, London.

—— 2001, 'The transformation of Italy, 225–28 BC', *Journal of Roman Studies* 91, 50–62.

—— 2003, 'Migration and the metropolis', in Edwards, C. and Woolf, G., eds, *Rome the Cosmopolis*, Cambridge, pp. 147–57.

—— forthcoming, 'Narrative economy', in Bang, P., Ikeguchi, M. and Ziche, H., eds, *New Approaches to the Ancient Economy*, Bari.

Morris, I., 1994, 'The ancient economy twenty years after The Ancient Economy', *Classical Philology* 89, 351–66.

—— 2002, 'Hard surfaces', in Cartledge, P., Cohen, E.E. and Foxhall, L., eds, *Money, Labour and Land: Approaches to the Economies of Ancient Greece*, London, pp. 8–43.

Mumford, L., 1961, *The City in History*, London.

Myres, J.L., 1930, *Who Were the Greeks?*, Berkeley, CA.

Nicolet, C., 1980, *The World of the Citizen in Republican Rome*, London.

Nietzsche, F., 1999, *The Birth of Tragedy and Other Writings*, eds R. Guess and R. Speirs, Cambridge.

Nippel, W., 1991, 'Introductory remarks: Max Weber's "The City" revisited', in Molho, A., Raaflaub, K. and Emlen, J., eds, *City States in Classical Antiquity and Medieval Italy*, Stuttgart, pp. 19–30.

Ober, J., 1989, *Mass and Elite in Democratic Athens: Rhetoric, Ideology and the Power of the People*, Princeton, NJ.

Parkin, T.G., 1992, *Demography and Roman Society*, Baltimore, MD.

Parkins, H., ed., 1997, *Roman Urbanism: Beyond the Consumer City*, London.

Parsons, T., 1964, *Essays in Sociological Theory*, New York.

Paz, O., 1970, *Claude Lévi-Strauss: An Introduction*, Ithaca, NY.

Pettifer, J., ed., 1999, *The New Macedonia Question*, London.

Polanyi, K., 1944, *The Great Transformation: The Political and Economic Origins of Our Time*, New York.

—— 1968, *Primitive, Archaic and Modern Economies: Essays of Karl Polanyi*, ed. G. Dalton, New York.

Pomeroy, S.B., 1975, *Goddesses, Whores, Wives, and Slaves: Women in Classical Antiquity*, New York.

—— 1991, *Women's History and Ancient History*, Chapel Hill, NC.

Ponting, C., 1991, *A Green History of the World: The Environment and the Collapse of Great Civilizations*, Harmondsworth, Middx.

Popper, K., 1952, *The Open Society and its Enemies*, London.

—— 1957, *The Poverty of Historicism*, London.

—— 1972, *The Logic of Scientific Discovery*, 3rd edn, London.

—— 1974, *Conjectures and Refutations: The Growth of Scientific Knowledge*, 5th edn, London.

Priest, S., 1991, *Theories of the Mind*, London.

Rackham, O., 1996, 'Ecology and pseudo-ecology: the example of ancient Greece', in Shipley, G. and Salmon, J., eds, *Human Landscapes in Classical Antiquity: Environment and Culture*, London, pp. 16–43.

Ranger, T. and Slack, P., eds, 1992, *Epidemics and Ideas: Essays on the Historical Perception of Pestilence*, Cambridge.

Rathbone, D.W., 1981, 'The development of agriculture in the Ager Cosanus during the Roman Republic: problems of evidence and interpretation', *Journal of Roman Studies* 71, 10–23.

von Reden, S., 1995, *Exchange in Ancient Greece*, London.

Reece, D.W., 1969, 'The technological weakness of the ancient world', *Greece & Rome* 16, 32–47.

Rosenberg, A., 1981, *Sociobiology and the Preemption of Social Science*, Oxford.

Rostovtzeff, M.I., 1926, *A History of the Ancient World*, Volume I, Oxford.

—— 1957, *The Social and Economic History of the Roman Empire*, 2nd edn, Oxford.

Sahlins, M., 1974, *Stone Age Economics*, London.

—— 1977, *The Use and Abuse of Biology: An Anthropological Critique of Sociobiology*, London.

Sallares, R., 1991, *The Ecology of the Ancient Greek World*, London.

—— 2002, *Malaria and Rome: A History of Malaria in Ancient Italy*, Oxford.

Scheidel, W., 2001, 'Progress and problems in Roman demography', in Scheidel, W., ed., *Debating Roman Demography*, Leiden, pp. 1–81.

Scheidel, W. and von Reden, S., eds, 2002, *The Ancient Economy*, Edinburgh.

Schiavone, A., 2000, *The End of the Past: Ancient Rome and the Modern West*, Cambridge, MA.

Scott, J., 1996, *Stratification and Power: Structures of Class, Status and Command*, Cambridge.

Scott, J.W., 1988, *Gender and the Politics of History*, New York.

—— 1991, 'Women's history', in Burke, P., ed., *New Perspectives on Historical Writing*, Cambridge, pp. 42–66.

Seager, W., 1999, *Theories of Consciousness: An Introduction and Assessment*, London.

Sennett, R., ed., 1969, *Classic Essays on the Culture of Cities*, New York.

Shaw, B.D., 1982, 'Social science and ancient history: Keith Hopkins in partibus infidelium', *Helios* 9.2, 17–57.

Shermer, M., 1997, *Why People Believe Weird Things: Pseudoscience, Superstition and Other Confusions of Our Time*, New York.

Shipley, G. and Salmon, J., eds, 1996, *Human Landscapes in Classical Antiquity: Environment and Culture*, London.

Simmons, I.G., 1993, *Environmental History: A Concise Introduction*, Oxford.

Singer, P., 1983, *Hegel*, Oxford.

Skinner, Q., ed., 1985, *The Return of Grand Theory in the Human Sciences*, Cambridge.

Spender, D., 1985, *Man Made Language*, 2nd edn, London.

Spengler, O., 1926, *The Decline of the West*, London.

de Ste Croix, G.E.M., 1981, *The Class Struggle in the Ancient Greek World from the Archaic Age to the Arab Conquests*, London.

Stannard, D.E., 1980, *Shrinking History*, Oxford.

Storr, A., 1989, *Freud*, Oxford.

Sturrock, J., 1986, *Structuralism*, London.

Tainter, J.A., 1988, *The Collapse of Complex Societies*, Cambridge.

Taplin, O., 1989, *Greek Fire*, London.

Tilley, C., ed., 1990, *Reading Material Culture: Structuralism, Hermeneutics and Post-structuralism*, Oxford.

Toner, J.P., 1995, *Leisure and Ancient Rome*, Cambridge.

Tong, R., 1989, *Feminist Thought: A Comprehensive Introduction*, London.

Tönnies, F., 1955, *Community and Association*, London.

Traugott, M., ed., 1978, *Émile Durkheim on Institutional Analysis*, Chicago.

Vernant, J.-P., 1980, *Myth and Society in Ancient Greece*, Hassocks, Sussex.

Veyne, P., 1985, 'Homosexuality in Ancient Rome', in Ariès, P. and Béjin, A., eds, *Western Sexuality: Practice and Precept in Past and Present Times*, Oxford, pp. 26–35.

Wall, D., 1994, *Green History: A Reader in Environmental Literature, Philosophy and Politics*, London.

Weber, M., 1930, *The Protestant Ethic and the Spirit of Capitalism*, London.

—— 1949, *The Methodology of the Social Sciences*, trans. E.A. Shils and H.A. Finch, New York.

—— 1968, *Economy and Society*, Volume I, eds G. Roth and C. Wittich, New York.

Webster, R., 1995, *Why Freud Was Wrong*, London.

Whittaker, C.R., 1990, 'The consumer city revisited: the vicus and the city', *Journal of Roman Archaeology* 3, 110–18.

—— 1993, 'Do theories of the ancient city matter?', in Whittaker, C.R., ed., *Land, City and Trade in the Roman Empire*, Aldershot, Surrey, section VI.

—— 1994, *The Frontiers of the Roman Empire: A Social and Economic Study*, Baltimore, MD.

Wilkins, J., Harvey, D. and Dobson, M., eds, 1995, *Food in Antiquity*, Exeter.

Williams, R., 1983, *Keywords: A Vocabulary of Culture and Society*, rev. edn, London.

Wills, C., 1996, *Plagues: Their Origin, History and Future*, London.

Wilson, E.O., 1975, *Sociobiology: The New Synthesis*, Cambridge, MA.

—— 1978, *On Human Nature*, Cambridge, MA.

Winkler, J.J., 1990, 'Laying down the law', in Halperin, D.M, Winkler J.J. and Zeitlin, F., eds, *Before Sexuality: The Construction of Erotic Experience in the Ancient Greek World*, Princeton, NJ, pp. 171–209.

Wollheim, R., 1971, *Sigmund Freud*, London.

Wood, E.M., 1988, *Peasant-Citizen and Slave: The Foundations of Athenian Democracy*, London.

—— 1995, *Democracy Against Capitalism: Renewing Historical Materialism*, Cambridge.

Woolf, G., 1997, *Becoming Roman: The Origins of Provincial Civilization in Gaul*, Cambridge.

Worster, D., 1988, *The Ends of the Earth: Perspectives on Modern Environmental History*, Cambridge.

Zivanovic, C., 1982, *Ancient Diseases: The Elements of Palaeopathology*, London.

Index

CPSIA information can be obtained
at www.ICGtesting.com
Printed in the USA
LVOW13s0110280217
525611LV00006B/397/P